Right Royal Remarks

From William I to Elizabeth II

Compiled by Michael Hill

ROBSON BOOKS

First published in Great Britain in 2003 by The Hovellers Press, 85 Beach Street, Deal, Kent

This edition published by Robson Books, The Chrysalis Building, Bramley Road, London, W10 6SP

An imprint of **Chrysalis** Books Group plc

The author has made every reasonable effort to contact all copyright holders. Any errors that may have occurred are inadvertent and anyone who for any reason has not been contacted is invited to write to the publishers so that a full acknowledgement may be made in subsequent editions of this work.

British Library Cataloguing in Publication Data
A catalogue record for this title is available from the British Library.

ISBN 1 86105 627 3

Typeset by SX Composing DTP, Rayleigh, Essex
Printed by Creative Print & Design (Wales), Ebbw Vale

Contents

Introduction

Everyone makes remarks but fortunately most people's blow away on the wind. Famous people find their remarks lasting a while in newspapers and magazines. Very famous people have their remarks retained, for better or for worse, in books and nowadays on film. Providentially the remarks of kings and queens tell us something not only about themselves but also about the age in which they lived. What may have appeared controversial at the time can often now be seen as more acceptable in the jigsaw of history. The royal remarks that follow should be read with that in mind.

Michael Hill

The House of Normandy

Normandy

1066–1154

William I
(Born 1027; reigned 1066–87)

Later known as 'The Conqueror', he was the son of the duke of Normandy with dubious claim to the English throne. Nevertheless his cross-Channel foray to Hastings in 1066 founded the Norman dynasty. A hard man but an able king, he instigated the Domesday Book of England, the forerunner of government surveys down the ages. Considerably overweight, he finally died when he fell off his horse in France.

..... 'I am therefore ready to risk my life against his in single combat to decide whether the kingdom of England should by right be his or mine.'
> *(Challenge to King Harold before the Battle of Hastings.)*

..... 'You fight not merely for victory but survival.'
> *(Call to his knights before the battle.)*

..... 'Look at me well, I am still alive.'
> *(Encouragement to his troops at a critical moment in the battle.)*

..... 'He could not have been a good one as he had not foreseen his own fate.'
> *(Ironic remark when told that his soothsayer had been killed during the battle.)*

..... 'I have not consented to pay fealty, nor will I now, because I never promised it nor do I find that my predecessors ever paid it to your predecessors. All things temporal and spiritual depend on my will.'

(Letter to Pope Gregory in 1075.)

..... 'I will light a hundred thousand candles at my Churching Mass.'

(Insulted about his fatness by Philip, King of France, in 1087 he invaded the Vexin and burnt the town of Mantes to the ground.)

..... 'I have forgiven him; let him not forgive himself so easily for bringing my old age with sorrow to the grave.'

(Speaking on his deathbed about his exiled eldest son Robert.)

William II
(Born 1056; reigned 1087-1100)

Although the second son of the 'Conqueror', he was bequeathed the English throne by his father. In constant rows with his nobles and particularly the Church, he was loathed by most of his subjects. The first gay monarch, he died mysteriously in the New Forest, shot by an arrow, probably as the result of a plot arranged by his younger brother Henry.

..... 'Pray as you please, I shall do as I please.'
> *(To the clergy who prayed that the king might be guided to appoint an archbishop of Canterbury in 1093.)*

..... 'By God's face, if you will not condemn him as I wish, I will condemn you.'
> *(To the barons at Rockingham Council to dismiss Archbishop Anselm whom he had himself recently appointed in 1093.)*

..... 'No predecessor of yours would have dared say such things to my father.'
> *(To Archbishop Anselm. William 'Rufus' had declared he would never endure an equal in his realm.)*

..... 'By the Holy Face of Lucca, if the bearer of this letter does not hasten to quit my dominion his eyes should be torn out.'
(After receiving a letter from Archbishop Anselm in Rome in 1095.)

..... 'That I might slay all the men of Wales.'
(Spoken prior to leading an army that captured barely one Welshman and suffered severe losses in the summer of 1097.)

..... 'Kings never drown.'
(Rejecting advice not to embark for France in an old, leaky ship at Southampton in 1099.)

..... 'He is a monk and has dreamed like one.'
(Scorning the warning of a monk who had dreamed the king was in danger; the next day William was killed.)

Henry I
(Born 1068; reigned 1100–35)

Youngest and only English-born son of William the Conqueror, he spent most of his reign fighting the French but he administered great and popular reforms in the law as well. Crafty, cruel and yet an able king, he was also something of a scholar. His only legitimate son, William, was drowned, leading once more to chaos in the kingdom.

..... 'I abolish all the evil practices with which the realm of England was unjustly oppressed.'

(At his coronation he repudiated the actions of his brother William II.)

..... 'I commit myself and the people of the whole kingdom of England to your counsel and to the counsel of those who with you ought to advise me.'

(Letter to Archbishop Anselm after his Coronation. Although there were few constitutional limits to royal power, prudent medieval kings found it advisable to consult the barons and leading churchmen on whose support they depended.)

..... 'An illiterate king is a crowned ass.'

..... 'For my own peace I will see no young men before dinner because they will waste time, and no old men after dinner because they will bore me.'

Stephen
(Born 1097; reigned 1135–54)

Grandson of the Conqueror, he usurped the throne and in his struggle to retain power allowed the kingdom to fall into sheer anarchy with the barons plundering at their pleasure. He was finally deposed by Henry (grandson of Henry I) and died at Dover. He was, in the words of G M Trevelyan, 'wholly unfit to be king'.

..... 'I will not have the child hung for all the gold in France.'
(Uncharacteristic gesture sparing a hostage, young William the Marshal, about to be executed.)

..... 'In the business of the kingdom I will work by the counsel of the Duke; but in the whole realm of England, as well as the Duke's part as my own, I will exercise royal justice.'
(The treaty signed at Winchester in 1153 when Duke Henry [the future Henry II] crossed from France and forced the king to appoint him heir to the English throne. Stephen died a year later.)

The House of Anjou

1154–1399

Henry II
(Born 1133; reigned 1154–89)

Grandson of Henry I by Matilda, he was a strong king who introduced the Common Law system but is probably best known for his incitement of the murder of Archbishop Becket. He married Eleanor of Aquitaine and ended up at loggerheads with their four sons. He died at Chinon in France.

..... 'That perfidious nation, on account of the favourable terms I received for their various transactions.'

(He tolerated the Jews.)

..... 'I order you to hold a free election, but, nevertheless, I forbid you to elect anyone except Richard my clerk, the Archdeacon of Poitiers.'

(Message to the monks of Winchester about their vacant bishopric in 1173. The king frequently left bishoprics vacant and pocketed the cash.)

..... 'I have nourished and raised up in my kingdom indolent and wretched fellows, faithless to their masters who they allow to be mocked so shamefully by a certain low-born clerk.'

(Example of the king's animosity towards Archbishop Becket.)

..... 'Who will rid me of this turbulent priest?'
(Outburst that led to the murder of Becket in Canterbury Cathedral in 1170.)

..... 'I call God to witness that I am extremely disturbed but more with anxiety about my reputation than qualms of conscience.'
(Letter to Pope Alexander II after the murder of Becket.)

..... 'St Thomas, guard for me my kingdom! To you I declare myself guilty of that [for] which others bear the blame.'
(To Richard of Ilchester when told in Normandy of the details of the death of Becket. He returned to England to do penance.)

..... 'You alone have proved yourself my lawful and true son; my other sons are really the bastards.'
(To his illegitimate son, Geoffrey, at Chinon in 1174.)

..... 'I have raised distinguished offspring to my own ruin.'
(At Chinon at the end of his life.)

..... 'The four eaglets are my four sons who cease not to persecute me even unto death. The youngest of them, whom I now embrace with so much affection, will sometime in the end insult me more grievously and more dangerously than any of the others.'
(The king had commissioned a painting in the royal palace at Winchester depicting the eaglets preying on the parent bird. The youngest son was John [later King John] who did desert his father in the war with France.)

14

..... 'May the Lord spare me until I have taken vengeance on you.'

(Whispered to his son Richard who had bent down to kiss him on his deathbed.)

Richard I
(Born 1157; reigned 1189–99)

Third son of Henry II, he was known as Coeur de Lion for his military prowess although a luckless Crusader. He spent a mere six months of his reign in England, was imprisoned and ransomed in Austria returning from Palestine, and was finally killed fighting in France. He married Berengaria, daughter of the king of Navarre, but left no direct heir.

..... '*Dieu et mon Droit*' ('God and my Right')
(Spoken before battle in France in 1189. Later on the Royal Arms of England.)

..... 'I would sell London if I could find anyone rich enough to buy it.'
(Seeking money to pay for his Crusade in 1190.)

..... 'Anyone who slays a man on board ship shall be thrown into the sea lashed to the corpse; if on land he shall be buried in the ground tied to the corpse . . . A convicted thief shall be shaved like a champion, tarred and feathered, and put ashore as soon as the ship touches land.'
(From the 'Articles of War' drawn up by the king at Chinon in 1190 before embarking on his Crusade.)

..... 'My brother John is not the man to conquer a country if there is anyone to offer even the feeblest resistance.'

(John had attempted to gain the throne when Richard was on a Crusade.)

..... 'Live, even if you do not want to, and on my bounty.'

(Chivalrous gesture by the king on giving a bag of gold to a French soldier who had shot at him with a crossbow during battle.)

..... 'By God's throat, even if that castle were all built of butter and not iron and stone, I have no doubt it would defend me against the King of France and all his foes.'

(About his new castle at Gaillard, France, in 1198.)

..... 'Thus we have defeated the King of France at Gisors but it is not we who have done it but God and our right through us.'

(The king's victory came only in the last year of his life, in 1198.)

John
(Born 1167; reigned 1199–1216)

Youngest son of Henry II, he was nicknamed 'Lackland' by his father because of a meagre inheritance. The reign of this furious little man was notable for the loss of all his French possessions. He improved civil administration but his tyranny finally incited the all-powerful barons to make him sign Magna Carta at Runnymede.

..... 'My peace should be inviolable even if granted to a dog.'
(A declaration.)

..... 'Now for the first time I am King of England.'
(Jubilant at the death of Archbishop Hubert Walter in 1205 who had opposed John's attempt to regain his lost French possessions.)

..... 'We will chase the red fox cub from his earth.'
(Threat to King Alexander of Scotland; one expedition resulted in the sacking of Berwick.)

..... 'These things we wished to be done publicly in London that our friends may rejoice and our enemies be openly confounded.'
(After signing a treaty in 1212 against France with the count of Flanders and the brother of the Emperor Otto.)

18

..... 'We command you to send us immediately, upon sight of these letters, ten pounds each of sulphur, tallow, gum and pitch, and four pounds of quicksilver; and if we stand in need of more to provide us therewith.'

(To Hubert de Burgh during the siege of La Roche-aux-Moines in 1214.)

..... 'Since I have become reconciled to God and submitted myself and my kingdom to the Church, nothing has gone well with me.'

(After news of the latest military disaster against the French in 1214.)

..... 'Why not ask for my kingdom?'

(Ironic reply to the demands of the barons in 1215 before signing Magna Carta.)

Henry III
(Born 1207; reigned 1216–72)

Eldest son of John, he succeeded his father at the age of nine. During his minority England was reasonably well governed but later years saw a return to the anarchy of the barons. The king's misrule led to the country's first 'Parliament' to represent boroughs under the influence of Simon de Montfort.

..... 'Welcome, sir. Truly I commit myself to God and to you, that for God's sake you may take care of me.'
(On accession, aged nine, to William the Marshal at Malmesbury in October 1216. They both then burst into tears.)

..... 'Servants do not judge their masters. Vassals do not judge their prince or bind him by conditions.'
(Reply to the baronial commission for granting money to the king in 1244.)

.....'May the devil give you safe conduct to Hell.'
(Dismissing Master Martin, a papal envoy seeking levies from English clergy in 1245.)

..... 'All these things shall I keep faithfully and undiminished as a man, as a Christian, as a soldier and as a king, crowned and anointed.'
(Taking an oath to uphold Magna Carta in 1253. He fell well short of the oath.)

..... 'It is no wonder that I covet money for it is dreadful to think of the debts in which I am involved. By God's head they amount to a sum of 200,000 marks. I am a mutilated and diminished king.'

(1255)

..... 'I know that if the treasure of Octavian were for sale, the City of London would purchase and suck it up; for these ill-bred Londoners who call themselves barons possess abundance even to a surfeit.'

..... 'I am Henry of Winchester, your King; do not harm me.'
(Unmilitary cry at the Battle of Evesham in 1265 after being wounded.)

Edward I
(Born 1279; reigned 1272–1307)

He was the eldest surviving son of Henry III. Able and energetic, he developed land law and summoned the first representative Parliament. However, he also banished all the Jews and campaigned with varying success against the Scots and Welsh. He married in turn the daughters of the kings of Castile and France.

..... 'By the pity of God I would rather speak with God than hear you talking about him.'
> *(The rebuke he, a religious man, once made to a priest.)*

..... 'heart, liver and lungs and all the interior of the said William out of which such perverse thoughts had proceeded, thrown into the fire and burnt.'
> *(Merciless to his enemies, he ordered Wallace, the Scottish leader, to be disembowelled.)*

..... 'By God, Sir Earl, you shall either go or hang.'
> *(To the earl of Norfolk in 1297 when he refused to lead an army to Gascony. The earl marshal did neither.)*

..... 'You know well how the King of France has beset my realm with a great fleet and a great multitude of warriors, and proposes if his power equal his unrighteous design to blot out the English tongue from the face of the earth.'

(The king's writ to summon the 'Model Parliament' in October 1295.)

..... 'You base-born whoreson, do you want to give away lands now, you who never gained any? As the Lord lives, if it was not for the breaking of the kingdom you should never enjoy your inheritance.'

(To his son Edward, Prince of Wales, who wished to bestow estates on his favourite, Piers Gaveston.)

..... 'hold counsel concerning matters which appertain to our crown or touch our person, our state or the state of our Council.'

(In 1281 the king forbade members of an ecclesiastical Provincial Council to do so.)

Edward II
(Born 1284; reigned 1307–27)

He was the eldest surviving son of Edward I. 'Unfit to govern', he lost disastrously to the Scots at Bannockburn, overindulged his favourite, Piers Gaveston, infuriated the barons, was forced to abdicate and was then brutally murdered in Berkeley Castle. He was unhappily married to Isabella, daughter of the king of France, who led the final rebellion to depose the king.

..... 'some of our bandy-legged harriers from Wales who may catch a hare if they find one asleep.'
(Sent to a friend in France, in 1305 when he was prince of Wales.)

..... 'howsoever this may rebound to my private disadvantage, as long as you shall stop persecuting my brother Piers, and allow him to have the Earldom of Cornwall.'
(In 1310 the king surrendered considerable powers to the barons. Two years later the barons broke their word and executed Gaveston.)

..... 'I have not forgotten the wrong that was done to my brother Piers.'

(Spoken to the earl of Lancaster at Berwick in 1319.)

..... 'Now would to God I were dead, so would to God I were.'

(Hounded across England by the forces of Queen Isabella to be imprisoned first at Kenilworth and then at Berkeley Castle.)

Edward III
(Born 1312; reigned 1327–77)

Eldest son of Edward II, he succeeded to the throne at the age of fourteen and although a patron of the arts and responsible for introducing 'Justices of the Peace' into the legal system, he spent most of his reign fighting – his mother, the Scots, the barons and particularly the French. Crécy and Poitiers were notable victories. His reign revealed the potential of the English longbow. 'In Edward III England once more found leadership equal to her steadily growing strength,' in the judgement of Winston Churchill.

..... 'The Kings of England have before these times been Lords of the English Sea on every side and it would very much grieve us if, in this kind of defence, our royal honour should (which God forbid) be lost or any way diminished in our time.'

(Royal instruction to his admirals on 18 August 1336.)

..... 'Ye and the archbishop have agreed to tell the same story to prevent my passage; though ye be unwilling, I will go, and ye who are afraid where there is nothing to fear, may remain at home.'

(Response to Admiral Sir Robert Morley and the archbishop of Canterbury who tried to dissuade the king from personally leading his ships against the 400-strong French fleet. At the ensuing battle off Sluys the French were soundly defeated.)

..... 'God, our hope, in a hard-fought conflict granted us to prevail, with no small slaughter of the enemy and the capture of nearly all the said fleet . . . and thus passage across the sea will thereafter be safer for our faithful people and many other benefits are likely to accrue therefrom . . . whereof the fairest hope already smiles.'

(Letter to his son Edward [the future Black Prince] after the Battle of Sluys.)

..... 'Honi soit qui mal y pense.' ('Evil be to him who evil thinks.')

(Spoken at a Court ball at Calais after the falling of the countess of Salisbury's garter. The Order of the Garter was founded by the king in 1348.)

..... 'Let the boy win his spurs.'

(Spoken about his son, the Black Prince, at the Battle of Crécy in 1346.)

..... 'Your people have devoured their horses, dogs and rats.'
(From the ultimatum from the king to the French king in 1347 after the year-long siege of Calais; the town remained English until 1558 in the reign of Mary I.)

..... 'I take this quarrel into my hand.'
(The king frequently took personal charge of lawsuits involving the kingdom's magistrates.)

..... 'Sweet son, God give you good perseverance. You are my son, for most loyally have you acquitted yourself this day. You are worthy to be a sovereign.'

(Spoken to the Prince of Wales, the Black Prince, after the great victory at Crécy. The Prince died in 1376, one year before his father.)

Richard II

(Born 1367; reigned 1377–99)

Grandson of Edward III and son of the Black Prince, he inherited the throne at the age of ten. His reign started well but upon his majority he became a tyrant, relied on favourites and introduced the dreaded poll tax, causing uprisings. He finally clashed with the barons and was deposed and murdered in Pontefract Castle.

..... 'Sir, will you shoot your King? I am your captain, follow me.'
Aged fourteen he rode out to face Wat Tyler's rebels at Smithfield outside London in 1381.

..... 'Villeins ye are and villeins ye shall remain.'
He soon reneged on his appeasing overtures.)

..... '[I] would not remove the meanest scullion of my kitchen at their bidding.'
(Replying to Parliament's request for a change of ministers in October 1386.)

'My God, a wonderful land is this and a fickle one; which hath exiled, slain, destroyed or ruined so many kings, rulers and great men, and is ever filled and toileth with strife and variance and envy.'

(In the Tower of London shortly before his death in 1400.)

'From the Devil we sprang and to the Devil we shall go.'

(Comment on his royal house; he was the last of the Norman kings though not of the house of Normandy. The French connection was ending.)

The House of Lancaster

1399–1461 and 1470–71

Henry IV
(Born 1367; reigned 1399–1413)

Grandson of Edward III, he usurped the throne from Richard II and subsequently fought the usual people: the Scots, Welsh, the French and the barons (including Harry Hotspur). An unstable king subject to epileptic fits. He married twice, once to an heiress, Mary de Bohun. He was the first king of the house of Lancaster.

..... 'If need be, Sir Thomas, I will in my own person ease thee of this office.'

(Having usurped the throne, the king addressed this remark at his coronation banquet to Sir Thomas Dymmoc, hereditary royal champion, meaning he was now de facto the new sovereign.)

..... 'This realm of England, and the crown with all the members and appurtenances, as I am descended by right line of the blood coming from the good lord Henry III; and through that right that God of his grace hath sent me, with the help of my kin and of my friends, to recover it; the which realm was in point to be undone for default of government and undoing of the good laws.'

(Spoken by the king on 30 September 1399 in Westminster Hall to the assembly to justify his claim to the throne.)

Henry V
(Born 1387; reigned 1413–22)

Eldest son of Henry IV. Well-read and a music lover as well as a brilliant soldier, he was, in Churchill's phrase, 'all that a king should be'. Legendary victories at Harfleur and Agincourt made him the virtual king of France; he was also the first king to send messages and letters home from the front in the English language. He married Catherine, daughter of the French king and died young, aged 35.

..... 'If God wills and I keep my life and health, in a few months I shall play such a ball-game with the French in their own courtyard that they will lose their fun in the end and win grief instead of the game.'
(Spoken to the French ambassador after receiving the insulting gift of tennis balls from the French king in 1414.)

..... 'If they labour to disturb us of our journey we shall escape their malice with honourable victory and great triumph.'
(During the march from Harfleur to Agincourt in October 1415.)

..... 'You speak like a fool, for by God is in Heaven . . . I should not wish to have even a single man more than I have now, if I could. For this is God's people . . . do you not believe that the Almighty with this small force of men on his side can conquer the hostile arrogance of the French who pride themselves on their numbers and their own strength?'

(Answering a doubter before the Battle of Agincourt.)

..... 'By the faith I owe God and St George, if they are not agreed by the time I have eaten my oysters they will both be hanged ere I have supped.'

(After summoning two warring northern lords to Windsor.)

..... 'I, Harry of Monmouth, shall small time reign and much get, and Harry born at Windsor shall long reign and all lose.'

(Henry V was right; his son Henry VI lost most of his French possessions.)

Henry VI
(Born 1421; reigned 1422–71)

Son of Henry V, he succeeded to the throne as a baby. Later a feeble and politically inept king, he had a long, ignominious reign that suffered the loss of the French possessions (thanks to Joan of Arc) and the start of that big baronial feud, the Wars of the Roses. The only lasting memorial of this sad, mad king was the foundation of Eton and King's College, Cambridge. He married the beautiful and dauntless Margaret of Anjou but their heir, Edward, Prince of Wales, was killed at the Battle of Tewkesbury in 1471, after which the deposed king was murdered in the Tower of London.

..... 'This truly, this is he unto whom we and our adversaries must yield and give over dominion.'
(*Prophetic words of the king on first meeting his young nephew, Henry Tudor, aged thirteen in 1470, the future Henry VII.*)

The House of York

1461–70 and 1471–85

Edward IV
(Born 1442; reigned 1461–83)

Descendant of Edward III, he continued the long-running Wars of the Roses, achieving a final decisive win at Tewkesbury in 1471. Having usurped the throne, he later authorised the murder of Henry VI, a prisoner in the Tower. Much given to debaucheries, he died suddenly at the age of 40, but was nevertheless the first king since Henry II to leave not debts but a fortune (mostly from confiscated Lancastrian lands). His imprudent marriage to Elizabeth Woodville and the ennoblement of eight of her relatives (at a time when there were only 80 peers in the kingdom) did not endear him to the barons.

..... 'I had three concubines which in three divers properties diversely excelled; one the merriest, another the wiliest, the third the holiest harlot of the realm, as one whom no man could get out of church lightly to any place but it were to his bed . . .'

Edward V

(Born 1470; reigned 1483)

He was the eldest son of Edward IV. The poor little lad, aged twelve, had a brief reign of 75 days before he and his brother, who had been confined in the Tower of London by the Lord Protector, his uncle, Richard, duke of Gloucester, were murdered.

..... 'Alas, I would my uncle would let me have my life yet, though I lose my kingdom.'
  (As one of the 'Princes in the Tower', shortly before his murder.)

Richard III
(Born 1452; reigned 1483–5)

Younger brother of Edward IV, he was generally considered a monster (particularly by Shakespeare) but, in Churchill's words, he did in fact 'inaugurate a series of enlightened reforms in every sphere of government'. His murderous behaviour ended at Bosworth in 1485 where he was the last English king to fall on the field of battle. His only son, the Prince of Wales, had died in 1484, leaving the throne open to the claims of Henry Tudor and the virtual end of the Middle Ages.

..... 'Ah, who shall a man trust? Those that I have brought up myself, those that I had weaned would most surely serve me, even those fail me and at my commandment will do nothing for me.'

> *(As Lord Protector in 1483, complaining that his orders to put to death the Princes in the Tower had not been carried out.)*

..... 'What? dost thou serve me with "ifs" and "ands"? I tell thee they have done it, and that I will make good upon thy body, traitor! . . . I will not dine until I have his head.'

> *(Addressing Lord Hastings in the Council Chamber, who was summarily beheaded in the Tower Yard in 1483.)*

..... 'That sorceress my brother's wife, and others with her – see how they have wasted my body with sorcery and witchcraft.')

(Continuing his outburst.)

..... 'An unknown Welshman whose father I never knew, nor him personally saw.'

(Dismissive comment on Henry Tudor in 1483.)

..... 'What punishment do they deserve who conspire against the life of one so nearly related to the King as myself, and entrusted with the government of the realm?'

(As Lord Protector to Edward V, his outburst of anger in the Council Chamber on 13 June 1485.)

..... 'The Earl of Richmond [Henry Tudor] be innocent and unwise because he temerariously attempted such a great enterprise with so small and thin a number of warlike persons.'

(Spoken on 10 August 1485, ten days before the Battle of Bosworth.)

..... 'Dismiss all fear . . . everyone give but one sure stroke and the day is ours. What prevaileth a handful of men to a whole realm? As for me, I assure you this day I will triumph by glorious victory or suffer death for immortal fame.'

(Spoken before the battle. He died fighting valiantly on the battlefield.)

..... 'Treason, treason, treason!'

(His last words, pace Shakespeare.)

42

The House of Tudor

Tudor

1485–1603

Henry VII
(Born 1457; reigned 1485–1509)

First Tudor king, he was a descendant of Edward III with slender claim to the throne when he seized the crown from Richard III at Bosworth. He united the houses of York and Lancaster by timely marriage to Elizabeth of York to establish the King's Peace after the Wars of the Roses. He brought stability and prosperity to the kingdom, limiting the perennial wars with France and Spain. An autocratic monarch, he was, according to Bacon, a politician's politician – clever, avaricious, fond of music and sport; but the realm profited from the King's sly, ruthless, unromantic efficiency.

..... 'That homicide and unnatural tyrant which now unjustly bears dominion over you.'
(As Henry Tudor, earl of Richmond, in a letter to muster his Welsh supporters against Richard III in 1483.)

..... 'If ever God gave victory to men fighting in a just quarrel He will this day send us triumphant victory.'
(To his troops on 22 August 1485 before Bosworth.)

..... 'That no manner of man rob or spoil no manner of commons coming from the field; but suffer them to pass home to their countries and dwelling-places with their horse and harness.'

(The new king's order after the Battle of Bosworth to let the combatants go unmolested.)

..... 'tender zeal for the wealth, security and defence of his subjects so that they could live in surety of their bodies according to my laws.'

(Stressing his concern for the establishment of the King's Peace in 1485.)

..... 'to carry bows, arrows, swords and weapons of invasion save when they should journey or ride.'

(The king forbade his subjects to do so.)

..... 'the robbing of churches, the ravishing of nuns and the taking of horse-meat without payment.'

(Adding a ban on such acts – even rumourmongers were to be pilloried.)

..... 'How the money goeth out of the realm? How to get it in again?' . . . Set the money at double the value that it goeth, foreigners will buy it and keep the Wool and Fell [leather] in the realm.'

(Financially shrewd, the king increased his income from £52,000 a year at the start of his reign to £142,000 a year at the end.)

..... 'My lords of Ireland, you will crown apes at last.'
(To dissident Irish nobles who had 'crowned' the Pretender, Lambert Simnel, in 1486. Instead of beheading Simnel, a former pastry cook, the king showed a sense of humour by confining him to the kitchens at Windsor.)

'Tell the Lords of Spain that the King will see the Princess even were she in bed.'
(The king was eager to see Catherine of Aragon, aged sixteen, who had just arrived in England to marry Arthur, Prince of Wales. Arthur died five months later and she was married off to his brother Henry, later Henry VIII, in 1501.)

'God hath left you a fair prince, two fair princesses; and that God is where He was, and that we are both young enough.'
(Queen Elizabeth of York's words of comfort to the king on the death of their son Arthur.)

'To avoid always damnable pomp and other outrageous superfluities.'
(Precise and thrifty instructions for his funeral in 1509.)

Henry VIII
(Born 1491; reigned 1509–47)

Second son of Henry VII, he began well as a talented, handsome, popular king but gradually became a tyrant, diseased, vengeful and frustrated after six marriages. He changed the course of English history by breaking with Rome over his divorce of Catherine of Aragon. Nevertheless his reign saw England become a great power with the opening up of new horizons both at home and overseas.

..... 'We are by the sufferance of God, King of England, and the Kings of England in times past never had any superior but God.'

(To Cardinal Wolsey in 1515.)

..... 'The King of France, is he as tall as I am? Is he as stout? What sort of a leg has he? He is indeed a worthy and honest sovereign but he is nevertheless a Frenchman and not to be trusted.'

(Spoken to the Venetian ambassador about his great rival, Francis I, in 1515.)

..... 'We are both young. If it is a daughter this time, by the Grace of God the sons will follow.'

(To Queen Catherine in 1516. No sons followed, which led to divorce and the breach with Rome.)

..... 'A venomous serpent . . . infernal wolf . . . detestable trumpeter of pride, calumnies and schism.'

(From his written attack on Martin Luther in 1521.)

..... 'I have now been above one whole year stricken with the dart of love.'

(Letter to Anne Boleyn in 1527.)

..... 'Who is she that will set her hands to work to get 3 pence a day when she can get at least 20 pence a day to sleep an hour with a friar, monk or priest.'

(From a pamphlet by the king attacking the monasteries in 1528.)

..... 'No more to you, at this present, mine own darling, for lack of time; but that I would you were in mine arms or I in yours; for I think it long since I kissed you. Written after killing of an hart at XI of the clock.'

(To Anne Boleyn in 1528, highlighting the two favourite royal pastimes.)

..... 'I have endured great agony debating with myself the contents of your letter, not knowing how to interpret them . . . I implore you to let me know plainly your feelings concerning the love that is between us.'

(To Anne Boleyn in 1528. She was refusing to become his mistress, holding out for marriage, which took place in 1533. She was beheaded in 1536.)

..... 'It drove me at last to consider the state of the Realm, and the dangers it stood in for lack of issue male to succeed me in this imperial dignity.'

(Dubious self-justification for the Anne Boleyn affair and the break with Rome.)

..... 'I perceive that that man hath the sow by the right ear; and if I had known this advice but two years ago, it had been in my way a great piece of money, and had also rid me out of much disquietness.'

(Letter to Edward Foxe in 1529 about Thomas Cranmer, archbishop of Canterbury, who arranged the king's divorce from Catherine of Aragon.)

..... 'If you neglect, stumble or shirk, we like a Prince of Justice will so entirely correct and punish you that the world shall take care of your example and beware.'

(Threat in 1529 to any subject who did not obey his break with the pope.)

..... 'We thought that the Clergy of our realm had been our subjects wholly, but now we have well perceived that they be but half our subjects, yea, and scarce our subjects.'

(To a delegation from Parliament about loyalty to the pope, 1532.)

..... 'Divine Providence hath mingled my joy with the bitterness of the death of her who brought me this happiness.'

(Letter to the French king, Francis I, in 1537 after the birth of his son, Edward, and the death of his beloved queen, Jane Seymour.)

..... 'My lord, if it were not to satisfy the world and my realm, I would not do that I must do this day for none earthly thing.'

(To Thomas Cromwell on the day of his disastrous marriage to Anne of Cleves, the 'Flanders Mare', in 1539.)

..... '[I] left her as good a maid as I found her.'

(His report to Thomas Cromwell the next day.)

..... 'There is no head in the kingdom so noble but I would make it fly.'

(To the duke of Norfolk and other dissident peers.)

..... 'Whatsoever offence or injury is offered to the meanest member of the House is to be judged as done against our person and the whole Court of Parliament.'

(To a deputation from the Commons, 1543.)

..... 'We be informed by our Judges that we at no time stand so high in our estate royal as in the time of Parliament when we as head and you as members are conjoined and knit together in one body politic.'

(Speech to the House of Commons in 1543.)

..... 'dark and inconvenient places to the encouragement of vice and sin and the high displeasure of God.'

(In 1544 actors were forbidden by the king to act in such places. They were allowed to act in the houses of nobles, Lord Mayors, etc.)

'I see and hear daily that you of the Clergy preach one gainst the other . . . some be too stiff in their old mumpsimus, others

51

be too busy and curious in their sumpsimus. Thus all men almost be in variety and discord.'

..... 'sack Leith and burn and subvert it and all the rest, putting man, woman and child to fire and sword without exception . . . and extend the like extremities and destructions in all towns and villages whereunto ye may reach conveniently.'

(The king's anger about suspected Scottish disloyalty is evident in his orders to Lord Hertford, the English commander, in 1544.)

..... 'I am sorry to know and hear how irreverently that most precious jewel, the Word of God, is disputed, rhymed, sung and jangled in every ale-house and tavern, contrary to the true meaning and doctrine of the same.'

(In a speech to Parliament in 1545.)

..... 'No Prince in the world more favoureth his subjects than I do you, nor no subjects or Commons more love and obey their Sovereign Lord than I perceive you do me. . .'

(To Parliament in 1545.)

..... 'I never spared men in my anger nor women in my lust.'

..... 'Tell that varlet Goswick that if he do not acknowledge his faith unto my lord of Canterbury . . . I will both make him a poor Goswick and otherwise punish him to the example of others.'

(Sir John Goswick had dared to criticise Archbishop Cranmer in the House of Commons.)

Edward VI
(Born 1537; reigned 1547–53)

The delicate and consumptive son of Henry VIII, he succeeded his father at the age of nine to be dominated by power-hungry politicians like Somerset and Dudley. An intelligent child, he showed interest in administration and economics and could converse in Latin and French; his reign saw England pass to complete Protestantism.

..... 'He will not die at this time for this morning I begged his life from God in my prayer and obtained it.'

    (A religious king, he made this comment in his journal about his tutor and friend Sir John Cheke who had been taken very ill.)

..... 'Methinks I am in prison. Here be no galleries nor no gardens to walk in.'

    (He disliked Windsor Castle because he had been taken there unwillingly by the Lord Protector, the duke of Somerset.)

..... 'For women, as far as ye may, avoid their company. Yet if the French King command you, you may sometime dance, so measure be your mean. Else apply yourself to riding, shooting or tennis with such honest games.'

    (Letter from the king, aged twelve, to his friend Barnaby Fitzpatrick, a young Irish noble.)

.....'If he were overthrown he would run through London and cry "Liberty! Liberty!" to raise the apprentices and rabble.'

(Reflecting in his journal on the behaviour of the duke of Somerset.)

..... 'The Duke of Somerset had his head cut off upon Tower Hill between eight and nine a clock in the morning.'

(A somewhat bleak entry in the king's journal in 1552 about his unloved Lord Protector.)

..... 'I would not set light God's will, thereby to please an Emperor.'

(Reply to requests from Charles V to tolerate the private Masses of the king's sister, Mary Tudor.)

..... 'Lord God, deliver me out of this miserable, wretched life.'

(Last words, on 6 July 1553.)

Mary I
(Born 1516; reigned 1553–8)

Elder daughter of Henry VIII by Catherine of Aragon, she might well have been a model Tudor sovereign, possessing virtue, courage, learning and intelligence. Her accession was greeted joyfully by the people yet after reigning for only five years she died hated and a tragic failure. The main reasons were her Roman Catholicism (she burnt some 300 Protestants) and her marriage to the king of Spain.

..... 'Priest.'
  (Her first, foreshadowing, word spoken, aged two, at the sight of her father's Venetian chaplain.)

..... 'Your humble servant to kiss the ground where you go, to be your dog on a string, your fish in a net, your bird in a cage, your humble trout.'
  (Love letter of Princess Mary, aged fourteen, to Francis Apsley, aged 23, in 1540.)

..... 'I am unworthy to suffer death in so good a quarrel. You should show more favour to me for my father's sake who made the more part of you out of nothing.'
  (As Princess Mary to a deputation of Councillors asking her to conform to the new Prayer Book in 1551.)

..... 'As for your new books, I thank God I never read any of them; I never did nor ever will do . . . My lord, for your gentleness to come and see me, I thank you; but for your offering to preach before me, I thank you never a whit.'

(As Princess Mary to Bishop Nicholas Ridley in 1551. He was burnt at the stake in 1556 when Mary was queen.)

..... '[Although you,] good sweet King, have more knowledge than any other of his years, yet it is not possible that he can be a judge in these things . . . Much less . . . can he in these years discern what is fittest in matter of divinity.'

(Letter to Edward VI, her brother, about the Prayer Book in 1551.)

..... 'It may please God that I might leave some fruit of my body behind to be your governor . . . and on the word of the Queen, I promise you, that if it shall not probably appear to all the nobility and commons . . . that this marriage shall be for the high benefit and commodity of the realm, then I shall abstain from marriage while I live.'

(To Parliament in 1553. She then did make the disastrous marriage in 1554 to King Philip of Spain, causing rebellion and the beginning of the persecution of Protestants that earned her the name of 'Bloody Mary'.)

..... 'I cannot tell how naturally the mother loveth the child for I was never the mother of any but certainly if a prince and governor may as naturally and earnestly love her subjects as the mother does the child, then assure yourselves that I, being your lady and mistress, do as earnestly and tenderly love and favour you, and I cannot but think that ye heartily and faithfully love me; and then I doubt not but that we shall give these rebels a short and speedy overthrow.'

(Courageous speech at Guildhall in 1554 during the Protestant uprising of the rebel Wyatt.)

..... 'You are to sit there, not as advocates for me, but as indifferent judges between me and my people.'

(Instructions to her judges to allow prisoners their legal rights.)

..... 'Not that only, but when I am dead and opened up you shall find Calais lying on my heart.'

(Calais had been captured by the French in 1558, the year of Mary's death.)

Elizabeth I
(Born 1533; reigned 1558–1603)

Daughter of Henry VIII and Anne Boleyn, she endured character-forming early years fraught with danger after her mother's execution. Queen at 25, she inherited from her father physical courage, hauteur, a fiery temper, an inclination to cruelty and a love of splendour; she could also be gracious, candid and kindly when she chose. Highly popular with her subjects, she had the invaluable faculty of selecting brilliant political advisers like Cecil and Walsingham, and sailors like Drake and Raleigh. The 'Golden Days' of Good Queen Bess saw England become a world power, particularly after the defeat of the Armada in 1588.

..... 'Inimical fortune, envious of all good and ever revolving human affairs.'

(First recorded written words, aged eleven, in 1544.)

..... 'This day died a man with much wit and very little judgement.'

(As Princess Elizabeth, aged fifteen, on the execution of her wayward guardian, Admiral Seymour, in 1548.)

..... 'Be ye well assured I will stand your good Queen.'

(At Temple Bar on the day before her Coronation, 14 January 1559.)

..... 'And Time hath brought me hither.'
(Exclamation at her Coronation, halting before an allegorical figure of Time. All her long life she was to be aware that Tudor England needed time to develop – in politics, finance, the arts, diplomacy, religion and commerce.)

..... 'This judgement I have of you . . . that you will be watchful to the state and that without respect of my private will you will give me that counsel that you think best.'
(To Sir William Cecil on his appointment as the queen's chief minister. He served her for almost her entire reign.)

..... 'Indeed I like silk stockings well because they are pleasant and fine and delicate, and henceforth I shall wear no more cloth stockings.'
(Spoken in the first year of her reign; previously her life had been necessarily frugal.)

..... 'We Princes are set as it were upon stages in the sight and view of the world.'
(Aged 25, at the beginning of her reign.)

..... 'I wish to confess to you and tell you my secret, which is, that I am no angel.'
(To the Spanish ambassador in 1560.)

..... 'You know the kingdom knows no kindred . . . where might is mixed with wit, there is too good an accord.'
(To Sir Henry Sydney about the threat posed by Mary, Queen of Scots (then married to Lord Darnley.)

..... 'The Queen of Scots is lighter of a fair son while I am but barren stock.'

(Possible reference in 1566 to Elizabeth's own seeming inability to have children.)

..... 'Mr Doctor, this loose gown becomes you mighty well; I wonder your notions be so narrow.'

(Rebuke to a Puritan divine at Oxford in 1566.)

..... 'Let this my discipline stand you in stead of sorer strokes, never to tempt too far a Prince's patience.'

(To Parliament on the subject of liberty in 1567.)

..... 'Let all men therefore bear their private faults; mine own have weight enough for me to answer for.'

(To Parliament in 1576.)

..... 'Look unto such men who of late have said that I was of no religion – neither hot nor cold, but such a one as one day would give God the vomit.'

(Order to her bishops to put down the Puritans.)

..... 'Proud prelate, you know what you were before I made you what you are. If you do not immediately comply with my request, I will unfrock you, by God!'

(To the bishop of Ely.)

..... 'I would fit him for heaven – but he would walk thither without a staff and leave his mantle behind him.'

(Rebuke to Bishop Aylmer whose sermon had displeased her.)

..... 'To be a king and wear a crown is a thing more glorious to them that see it than it is pleasant to them that bear it.'

..... 'To satisfy you, I have already joined myself in marriage to a husband, namely the Kingdom of England.'
(Answering a parliamentary plea that she should marry.)

..... 'Be of good cheer, for you will never want. For the bullet was meant for me.'
(To one of her bargemen wounded by a gun fired from the shore. She gave the man her own handkerchief.)

..... 'There is only one Jesus Christ and all the rest is a dispute over trifles.'
(The queen had no patience with those who wanted to go to war over the minutiae of theological dogma.)

..... 'I think that at worst, God has not yet decided that England shall cease to stand where she does.'

..... 'Good morning, gentlemen both.'
(A quip to a delegation of eighteen tailors.)

..... 'I suppose few that be not professors have read more.'
(To Parliament in 1585. The queen had read widely, could speak six languages and had translated Xenophon, Tacitus and Horace.)

..... 'If I were turned out of my realm in my petticoat I were able to live any place in Christendom.'

..... 'God's death! My Lord, I will have but one mistress and no master.'

(To the earl of Leicester, her reputed lover.)

..... 'For God's sake regard your surety against the wicked suggestion of the Jesuits who make it an acceptable sacrifice to God . . . that a King not of their profession should be murdered.'

(Letter to James VI of Scotland.)

..... 'My commissioners behave to me as strawberry vendors do to their customers who lay two or three great strawberries at the mouth of the pottle [basket] and all the rest are little ones; so they give me two or three good prices at the first and the rest fetch nothing.'

(Complaint about the poor returns from the sale of Crown lands. The queen was always parsimonious.)

..... 'And you, Madam, I may not call you, and Mrs I am ashamed to call you, so I know not what to call you, but yet I thank you.'

(Addressing the wife of Archbishop Parker after she had been 'greatly feasted'. The queen disapproved of married clergy.)

..... 'O let Thine enemies know that Thou has received England . . . into Thy own protection. Set a wall about it, O Lord, and evermore mightily defend it.'

(From a prayer composed by the queen during the Spanish Armada battle in the Channel in 1588.)

..... 'Let tyrants fear . . . I am come among you, as you see, at this time, not for my recreation and disport but being resolved in the midst and heat of the battle to live and die among you all . . . I know I have the body of a weak and feeble woman but I have the heart and stomach of a King and of a King of England too . . . I myself will take up arms, I myself will be your general, judge and recorder of every one of your virtues in the field.'

(From her famous speech to the troops at Tilbury on 9 August 1588 during the approach of the Armada.)

..... 'Rather a jest than a victory.'

(Scornful comment on a military escapade of the earl of Essex in France in 1591.)

..... 'The Prince's prerogative and the subject's privilege are solid felicities together but empty notions asunder.'

(Reply to criticism of the Crown's right to grant monopolies in 1601.)

..... 'And though God hath raised me high, yet this I account the glory of my crown, that I have reigned with your loves . . . though you have had and may have Princes more mighty and wise sitting in this seat, yet you never had nor shall have any that will be more careful and loving.'

(From her 'Golden Speech' to the House of Commons in 1601.)

..... 'Little man, little man, the word must is not to be used to Princes.'

(To Sir Robert Cecil, her chief minister, when he said she must go to bed during her final illness.)

..... 'My lord, I am tied with a chain of iron about my neck.'
(The dying queen to Lord Charles Howard at Richmond in 1603.)

The House of Stuart

Stuart

1603–1714

James I
(Born 1566: reigned 1603–25)

Son of Mary, Queen of Scots, he became James VI of Scotland at the age of fifteen and the first Stuart king of England at 37. Famously known as the 'wisest fool in Christendom', he was alledged to have three obsessions: hunting, learning and young men. He ruined what might have been a reasonable reign by indulging favourites like Somerset and Buckingham, and tolerating financial fiddles. He was married to the extravagant Princess Anne of Denmark.

..... 'Many a man speaks of Robin Hood who never shot his bow.'

(Somewhat crude defence of the use of 'with my body I thee worship' in his marriage ceremony to Princess Anne of Denmark in 1589.)

..... 'An old, experienced king, needing no lessons.'

(Optimistic remark on arriving in England from Scotland in 1603 to assume the Crown.)

..... 'A king without state, without order, where beardless boys would brave me to my face.'

(Rather different reference to his reign as James VI of Scotland.)

..... 'The state of monarchy is the supremest thing upon earth; for kings are not only God's Lieutenants upon earth and sit upon God's throne but even by God himself are called gods.'
(Explicit statement of Divine Right to his first Parliament in 1604.)

..... 'A custom loathsome to the eye, hateful to the nose, harmful to the brain, dangerous to the lungs, and in the black, stinking fume thereof, resembling the horrible Stygian smoke of the pit that is bottomless.'
(From his 'A Counterblast to Tobacco' 1604.)

..... 'If you aim at a Scottish Presbytery it agreeth as well with a monarchy as God and the Devil. Then Jack and Tom and Will and Dick shall meet and at their pleasure censure me and my council and all our proceedings . . . No Bishop, no King! If this be all your party hath to say, I will make them conform themselves or else will harry them out of the Kingdom.'
(Addressing the Puritans at the Hampton Court Conference in 1604. The king did, however, encourage the new translation of the Bible on which they were working.)

..... 'I give not a turd for your preaching.'
(To a Presbyterian minister.)

..... 'It should never have been spoken or written in ages succeeding that I had died ingloriously in an Ale-house, a stews or such vile place, but that mine end should have been with the most honourable and best company.'
(Somewhat silly speech to Parliament after the Gunpowder Plot in 1605 implying that he would have been glad to have been blown up with the MPs.)

..... 'I am the husband and all the whole Isle is my wife.'
(As king of the Scots he desired union between the two countries. This was turned down by the Commons in 1607 – but achieved exactly 100 years later under Queen Anne.)

..... 'I could rather have wished with Job never to have been born than that glorious sun of my entry should have been so soon overcast with the dark clouds of irreparable misery.'
(To Parliament in 1610 during the usual arguments about money.)

..... 'I am surprised that my ancestors should have permitted such an institution to come into existence.'
(After dissolving the Addled Parliament in 1614.)

..... '[It be] presumption and high contempt in a subject to dispute what a king can do, or say that a king cannot do this or that.'
(In the Star Chamber in 1616.)

..... 'I, James, am neither God nor an angel but a man like any other. You may be sure that I love the Earl of Buckingham more than anyone else . . . for Jesus Christ did the same, and therefore I cannot be blamed. Christ had his John and I have my George.'
(Defence of his infatuation with George Villiers [later duke of Buckingham] to the Lords of the Council in 1617.)

..... 'The common and meaner sort would go in disgust to ale-houses and there indulge in a number of idle and discontented speeches.'
(Justification for legalising Sunday sports against the wishes of the Puritans in 1618.)

..... 'He was a bold man who first swallowed an oyster.'
(Quoted by Jonathan Swift.)

..... 'I am resolved that two religions should not lie in my bed.'
*(Prince Henry, his son, on a proposed marriage to a
French Catholic.)*

.....'You will live to have your bellyfull of Parliaments.'
(To his son Charles, the future Charles I.)

..... 'God's wounds! I will pull down my breeches and they
shall also see my arse.'
*(After being told that the English people wished occasionally to see
his face; he spent most of the year hunting in the royal forests.)*

..... 'Go to Hell or Connaught!'
*(Jibe to unruly courtiers; Connaught was considered the most
primitive and remote of Irish provinces.)*

..... 'A spice of envy hath made all my speeches heretofore
turn like spittle in the wind upon mine own face.'
(Speech to Parliament in 1621.)

70

Charles I

(Born 1600; reigned 1625–49)

Son of James I, he was a better art patron than a politician. At loggerheads with Members of Parliament from the start of his reign, he attempted to rule without them, which ultimately led to the Civil War of 1642–6. Losing to Cromwell and the 'Roundheads', he was tried and died bravely on the scaffold in 1649. He made a politically imprudent but personally happy marriage to the French Catholic princess, Henrietta Maria.

..... 'Sire, I stand on mine own two feet; I have no helps by art; thus high am I, neither higher nor lower.'

(Said to Charles as Prince of Wales by his bride-to-be, the sixteen-year-old Princess Henrietta Maria, sister of the king of France, to show that although small she was not wearing high-heeled shoes in 1625.)

..... 'Parliaments are altogether in my power for the calling, sitting and dissolution. Therefore as I find the fruits of them to be good or evil, they are to continue or not to be.'

(To Parliament in 1625.)

..... 'I command you, send all the French away tomorrow out of the town. If you can by fair means (but stick not long in disputing), otherwise force them away, driving them away like so many wild beasts.'

(Orders to the duke of Buckingham, his favourite, to dismiss all the young queen's French servants in 1626.)

..... 'Now that you have all things according to your wishes, and I am so far engaged that you think there is no retreat, now you begin to set the dice and make your own game. But I pray you be not deceived, it is not a Parliamentary way nor is it a way to deal with a King.'

(Aggressive speech to the Lords and Commons in 1626, mainly over their attitude to the duke of Buckingham.)

..... 'Take not this as threatening, for I scorn to threaten any but my equals.'

(Tactless remark to his third Parliament in 1628.)

..... 'The middle way between the pomp of superstitious tyranny and the meanness of fantastic anarchy.'

(Description of the English Church in 1633.)

..... 'Never make a defence of apology before you be accused.'

(Letter to Lord Wentworth in 1636.)

..... 'Well, since I see all the birds are flown I do expect from you that you shall send them unto me as they return hither. If not, I will seek them myself, for their treason is foul and such a one as you will thank me to discover.'

(To the Speaker after the king's invasion of the House of Commons

to arrest and impeach five MPs (including Pym and Hampden) in January 1642. His action evoked the famous reply from the Speaker, William Lenthall: 'May it please your Majesty, I have neither eyes to see nor tongue to speak in this place but as this House is pleased to direct me, whose servant I am.')

..... 'You have taken the Government almost to pieces and, I may say, it is almost off its hinges. A skilful watchmaker, to clean his watch, takes it asunder and when it is put together, it will go better; but just remember if you leave out one pin the watch may be worse and not better.'

(To Parliament in 1641 reluctantly assenting to the Triennial Act requiring a new Parliament every three years.)

..... 'What seems at first but a handbreadth, by seditious spirits as by strong winds are soon made a cover and darken the whole heaven.'

(Laying blame on the Presbyterians for the outbreak of the Civil War in 1642.)

..... 'The nature of Presbyterian government is to steal or force the Crown from the King's Head.'

(Letter to the queen in 1646.)

..... 'There never was a man so alone as I, and therefore very much to be excused for the committing of any error because I have reason to suspect everything that these advised me, and to distrust mine own single opinion, having no living soul to help me.'

(Letter to the queen in 1646 after the final battle of the Civil War at Naseby.)

73

..... 'I conjure you, by your unspotted faithfulness, by all that you love, by all that is good, that no threatenings, no apprehension of danger to my person make you stir one jot from any foundation in relation to that authority which the Prince of Wales is born to.'

(Letter to the queen – in France with the Prince of Wales – before the king surrendered to the Scots in 1646).

..... 'People are governed by the pulpit more than the sword in time of peace.'

..... 'To conclude, if God gives you success, use it humbly and far from revenge. If he restores you to your right upon hard conditions, whatever you promise, keep . . . We do not more affectionately pray for you than we do that the ancient glory and renown of this nation be not buried in irreligion and fanatic humour.'

(Letter to Charles, Prince of Wales, in 1648.)

..... 'They will cut off my head and perhaps make thee King; but mark what I say, you must not be King so long as your brothers, Charles and James do live.'

(Letter to Prince Henry, aged eight, in 1649. The child bravely replied, 'I will be torn in pieces first.')

..... 'On the contrary, the authority of obedience unto kings is clearly warranted and strictly commanded in both Old and New Testaments, which if denied, I am ready instantly to prove.'

(In his defence at his trial in 1649.)

..... 'Remember, I am your King, your lawful King, and what sins you bring upon your heads and the judgement of God on this land.'

(At his trial in 1649.)

..... 'How can any free-born subject of England call life or anything he possesseth his own if power without right daily make new and abrogate the old fundamental laws of the land?'

(At his trial in 1649.)

..... 'I am not suffered to speak. Except what justice other people will have.'

(Last words at his trial after sentence of death.)

..... 'Never repose so much upon any man's single counsel, fidelity and discretion in managing affairs of the first magnitude (that is, matters of religion and justice) as to create in yourself or others a diffidence of your own judgement.'

(Letter to his son Charles, shortly before his execution in 1649.)

..... 'A subject and a Sovereign are clean different things . . . If I would have given way to an arbitrary way, for to have all laws changed according to the Power of the Sword, I needed not to have come here; and therefore I tell you . . . that I am the Martyr of the People.'

(Speech from the scaffold, 30 January 1649.)

..... 'Death is not terrible to me; I bless God I am prepared . . . I am going from a corruptible to an incorruptible crown where no disturbance can be.'

(On the scaffold.)

Charles II
(Born 1630; reigned 1660–85)

Eldest son of Charles I, he fled from England after losing to Cromwell at the Battle of Worcester in 1651, subsequently living an impoverished and dissolute life on the Continent. Returning as king in 1660, the 'Merry Monarch' achieved the remarkable feat of fathering fourteen children without producing a legitimate heir by his wife, Catherine of Braganza. Sex apart, he was a competent monarch, reviving the Exchequer and the Royal Navy to leave a prosperous England. Despite the usual Stuart rows with Parliament he oversaw the introduction of Habeas Corpus (literally 'you must have the body'), which might well serve as his private epitaph.

..... 'I think I must repent, too, that ever I was born.'
(Ironic comment of the king after listening to a catalogue of his sins before being crowned in Scotland in 1651.)

..... 'So we fell a-running both of us, up the lane as long as we could run, it being very deep and very dirty.'
(Describing his escape, aged 22, after the Battle of Worcester in 1651; he then hid in the famous oak tree.)

..... 'We pass our lives as well as people can do that have no money, for we dance and play as if we had taken the Plate Fleet.'
  (In exile in southern Germany in the 1650s. The Plate Fleet were the ships that carried Spain's silver from its mines in America.)

..... 'Odd's fish, they are all dull and foggy.'
  (His opinion of the German princesses suggested as his bride.)

..... 'I am now going to take my usual physic at tennis.'
  (As king in 1660 to the Lord Chancellor about his regular game at 8 a.m.)

..... 'Oh, then 'tis, oh, then I think there's no Hell/Like loving too well.'
  (Lines from a poem he wrote to woo Frances Stuart 'La Belle Stuart' in 1662. He was not successful)

..... 'If you are well acquainted with a little fantastical gentleman called Cupid as I am, you would neither wonder nor take ill any sudden changes which do happen in the affairs of his conducting.'
  (Letter to his sister when the duke of Richmond married his favourite, Frances Stuart, in 1662.)

..... 'It was happy for the honour of the nation I was not put to the consummation of the marriage last night, for I was so sleepy, by having slept two hours in my journey, that I was afraid that matters would have gone very sleepily.'
  (On his first meeting with Princess Catherine of Braganza at Portsmouth in 1662.)

..... 'I cannot tell you how happy I think myself and must be the worst man living (which I think I am not) if I am not a good husband.'

(Optimistic remark to Lord Clarendon after his marriage to Catherine of Braganza in 1662.)

..... 'You will have heard of our taking New Amsterdam which lies just by New England. 'Tis a place of great importance to trade. It did belong to England heretofore but the Dutch by degrees drove our people out and built a very good town, but we have got the better of it and 'tis now called New York.'

(Letter to his sister in 1664.)

..... 'I am very glad that your indisposition of health is turned into a great belly [but] am afraid your shape is not so advantageously made for that convenience as hers is; however, a boy will recompense two grunts or more.'

(Typically frank letter to his sister Minette [Mary of Orange], about to give birth. 'Hers' refers to the king's mistress, the duchess of Portsmouth, who had just produced a girl in 1665.)

..... 'It is upon the Navy under the Providence of God that the safety, honour and welfare of this realm do chiefly attend.'

(Articles of War issued in the King's name in 1666.)

..... 'You little bastard.'

(Affectionate name of Nell Gwynn for her son by the king. When the king protested she replied, 'Why, I have nothing else to call him.' He was created duke of St Albans.)

..... 'Not a religion for a gentleman.'

(Comment on Presbyterianism.)

..... 'Better than a play!'
(Comment on the Divorce debate in the House of Lords.)

..... 'My words are my own and my actions are my ministers.'
(Reply to Lord Rochester's quip that the king 'Never said a foolish thing, Nor ever did a wise one.')

..... 'Now, nephew, to your work! Hey! St George for England!'
(Characteristic remark by the king as he drew the bedcurtains round Prince William of Orange and his niece Mary – the future William and Mary – on their wedding night in 1677.)

..... 'I will submit to anything rather than endure the gentlemen of the Commons any longer.'
(After dissolving Parliament in 1679 over the Bill to exclude his brother James from the throne.)

..... 'You better have one king than five hundred.'
(After dissolving Parliament in 1681.)

..... 'I've tried him drunk and I've tried him sober and there's nothing in him.'
(About Prince George of Denmark, husband of Princess Anne, daughter of the duke of York, the king's brother in 1683.)

..... 'We talk here of going to tea, of going to Winchester, and everything else except sitting still all summer which was the height of my ambition.'
(Prince George of Denmark [see above] in 1685.)

79

..... 'I am weary of travelling, I am resolved to go abroad no more. But when I am dead and gone I know not what my brother will do; I am much afraid that when he comes to the crown he will be obliged to travel again.'
(To Sir Richard Bulstrode in 1683. The king proved right; James II was deposed in 1688 and fled to France.)

..... 'All appetites are free and God will never damn a man for allowing himself a little pleasure.'
(To the bishop of Salisbury in 1685.)

..... 'Never in the way and never out of it.'
(About his Lord Treasurer, Sydney Godolphin.)

..... 'foretell the winners.'
(An astrologer who offered his services to the king, was taken to Newmarket and asked to do the above.)

..... 'Let not poor Nelly starve.'
(Deathbed request about Nell Gwynn. On one occasion the mob mistook her for the king's French Catholic mistress, the duchess of Portsmouth. 'Be civil, good people,' shouted Nell from her coach, 'I am the Protestant whore,' much to the delight of the crowd.)

..... 'I am sorry, gentlemen, for being such an unconscionable time a-dying.'
(During his final illness in 1685.)

..... 'Open the curtains that I may once more see day.'
(Last words, 6 February 1685.)

James II

(Born 1633; reigned 1685–8; died 1701)

Brother of Charles II and something of a disaster, he attempted to restore Catholicism to England and to overthrow the Constitution, both of which finally led to his own deposing by his son-in-law, William of Orange, and his death in exile in France. He married twice, fathering the future Queens Mary and Anne, and also Prince James Edward, the Old Pretender.

..... 'The examples of the late King, my father, and the King, my brother, who had weakened this authority – and in my father's case brought on his own death – were by too great a display of leniency.'

(Spoken as duke of York in 1680 during the Exclusion Bill crisis, which aimed to exclude him, as a Catholic, from the throne.)

..... 'I entreat you to interest yourself no more for a prince so unfortunate, but permit me to withdraw with my family to some corner of the world where I may cease to be an interruption to your Majesty's usual course of prosperity and glory.'

(Bitter letter to the king of France after James's defeat at the Battle of the Boyne, his attempt to regain his throne in 1690.)

..... 'A vast conspiracy of the ill-intentioned.'
(Comment to the pope's envoy about Parliament in 1686.)

..... 'He is younger than I but I have much less control.'
(Envy of the French King Louis XIV's sexual continence. James had been forced by the Jesuits to give up his Protestant mistress, Catherine Sedley.)

..... 'I fear those in Whitehall more than my foreign enemies.'
(Spoken to the papal nuncio a fortnight before William of Orange landed at Torbay in 1688.)

..... 'God help me! Even my children have forsaken me!'
(Reaction to the news that his daughter Anne (the future Queen Anne) had fled from London to join her sister Mary and William of Orange in 1688.)

..... 'If I could have relied upon all my troops I might not have been put to this extremity I am in.'
(To Lord Feversham on 10 December 1688, on the night before the king fled from London to France. The duke of Marlborough had taken his troops over to William of Orange.)

..... 'If I had agreed to live quietly and treat my religion as a private matter . . . I could have been one of the most powerful kings ever to reign in England.'
(Dubious boast after his flight to France in 1688.)

William III &
Mary II

(William born 1650;
reigned 1688–1702
Mary born 1662; reigned 1688–94)

Eldest daughter of James II, Mary married Dutch William and together they deposed her father. Unlike his wife, William was never popular with his subjects and after her death he spent half the year abroad. To his credit he can claim to have established a form of constitutional monarchy, the Bank of England and the National Debt. He was probably gay.

..... 'I cannot leave the battlefield nor believe it would be agreeable for a lady to be where the battlefield is.'
(William of Orange's reply to Charles II's suggestion that he might marry his niece, Mary, in 1674. He did so in 1677.)

..... 'My heart is not made for a kingdom and my inclination leads me to a retired life.'

(Mary, at the start of her reign.)

..... 'Very much neglected, little respected, censured by all, commended by none.'
(Mary's view of herself in the early part of her reign. In fact when she died aged 32 she was greatly loved and respected – unlike her husband.)

..... 'I have not come to establish a republic or be a Duke of Venice . . . I will not be my wife's gentleman usher.'
(William to the Lords, demanding the title of King in 1689.)

..... 'The Commons used me like a dog.'
(William's comment to Lord Halifax about the limitations of his joint-rule with Mary in 1689.)

..... 'I must hear of business which being a thing I am so new in and so unfit for does but break my brains the more and not ease the heart.'
(Mary, reluctantly presiding over the Regency Council while William was abroad in 1690.)

..... '[I find] general peevishness and silliness in them all except Lord Sidney.'
(A later remark by Mary about members of the Regency Council.)

..... 'It seems to me very extraordinary that it should be impossible to have esteem and regard for a young man without it being criminal.'
(William about his friendship with Keppel, one of his pages in 1691, who was later created earl of Albemarle.)

..... 'During the course of our marriage I have never known one single fault in her.'
(William to Bishop Burnett after the death of Mary in 1694.)

..... 'There is one certain means by which I can be sure never to see my country's ruin: I will die in the last ditch.'
(William during the Dutch war with France.)

..... 'Every bullet has its billet.'
(William during the war with France.)

..... 'He, Professor Dodwell, has set his heart on being a martyr and I have set mine on disappointing him.'
(William's remark about a Jacobite.)

Anne

(Born 1665; reigned 1702–14)

Sister of Mary II and the 'quintessence of ordinariness', she married a dim Danish prince by whom she had seventeen children, all of whom died. She was able to enjoy the great duke of Marlborough's victories (Blenheim, Ramillies, Oudenarde and Malplaquet) but was continually beset by quarrelling politicians. She was the last of the wayward Stuarts.

..... 'The more I see of these fooleries and the more I hear of that religion, the more I dislike it.'
(As Princess Anne, aged fifteen, on Roman Catholicism.)

..... 'I should be unfortunate to be out of town when the Queen was brought to bed for I shall never now be satisfied whether the child be true or false. It may be it is our brother but God only knows.'
(Princess Anne to her sister Mary in 1688 about the wife of James II who had given birth to Prince James, the Old Pretender.)

..... 'As I know my heart to be entirely English, I can very sincerely assure you that there is not one thing you can expect or desire of me which I shall not be ready to do for the happiness or prosperity of England.'
(As queen, giving her well-received first address to Parliament and including an opening dig at William of Orange in 1702.)

86

..... 'It means I'm growing old when ladies declare war on me.'

> *(Quip by Louis XIV when England declared war on France two months after Anne's accession.)*

..... 'I have the same opinion of Whig and Tory that I ever had. I knew their principles very well and when I know myself to be in the right, nothing can make me alter mine.'

> *(Letter about Lord Sunderland, Secretary of State, in 1705.)*

..... 'We four must never part till death mows us down with his impartial hand.'

> *(To Sarah, duchess of Marlborough about herself, her husband Prince George of Denmark and the Great Duke. It was not to be, owing mainly to the behaviour of the duchess.)*

..... 'I want words to express the joy I have that you are well after your glorious success for which, next to God Almighty, my thanks are due to you; and indeed I can never say enough for all the great and faithful services you have done me.'

> *(To the duke of Marlborough after the Battle of Oudenarde in 1708.)*

..... 'I have changed my ministers but I have not changed my measures; I am still for moderation and will govern by it.'

> *(To the new Tory cabinet in 1711.)*

..... '[I urge you] To prefer your own brother, the last male of our name, to the Duchess of Hanover, the remotest relation we have, whose friendship you have no reason to rely on or to be fond of and who will leave the government to foreigners of another language.'

(Letter from Prince James, the Old Pretender, to Queen Anne in 1712, putting his case for succeeding her.)

..... 'He neglected all business; he was seldom to be understood; when he did explain himself I could not depend upon the truth of what he said; he never came to me at the appointed time; he often came drunk; lastly, to crown all he behaved himself towards me with ill manner, indecency and disrespect.'

(Reasons for dismissing her Lord Treasurer, Robert Harley, in 1714.)

The House of
Hanover

1714–1901

George I
(Born 1660; reigned 1714–27)

The 54-year-old Elector of Hanover, a small, choleric German prince, he succeeded to the English throne as the great-grandson of James I. Already divorced from his wife, he arrived in London with predatory mistresses and able German advisers. An indolent king who spoke no English, he took little part in the government of the country, which was fortunately in the hands of a brilliant political manager, Robert Walpole. Like all future Hanoverians he was perpetually at odds with his eldest son. The king's heart remained in Hanover but by being a constitutional figurehead he unintentionally served his adopted country well.

..... 'My dear Duke, I hope you have now seen the end of your troubles.'

(On his arrival in London as king in September 1714 he greeted the duke of Marlborough who had been dismissed from public office by Queen Anne. Since George I could speak no English and his ministers no German, most conversations were carried on in French.)

..... 'Votre conduite . . . Votre conduite.'

(One of few remarks made by the king to the Prince of Wales when at an attempt at reconciliation the embarrassed Prince knelt at his enraged father's feet. They loathed each other.)

..... 'Cette diablesse Madame la Princesse.'
      (His not entirely unfriendly name for the Princess of Wales.)

..... 'I hate all Boets and Bainters.'
      (A rare attempt at the English language.)

..... '[I] looked upon them all as king-killers and Republicans, and grudged them their riches as well as their liberty.'
      (Expressing his distrust of his English subjects.)

George II
(Born 1685; reigned 1727–60)

The eldest son of George I. 'Like his father,' wrote Sir John Plumb, 'George was stupid but complicated.' Unlike his father he was quite active in affairs of state, although easily bullied first by his wife Caroline and then by Walpole and William Pitt. He was the last English king to command troops in the field, being present at the Battle of Dettingen. In fact twenty years of war did much to boost Britain's economy and the king's reign closed in a blaze of military glory: Wolfe's success in Canada, Clive's in India and victory over the French at Minden. On the domestic side he and Queen Caroline spent much time loathing their son, the Prince of Wales.

As Prince of Wales, at the christening of his son he was so enraged by George I's appointment of the duke of Newcastle as a godparent that he growled at the duke, 'Rascal, I find you out.' Confused by the Prince's anger and German accent, the duke thought he said, 'I'll fight you.' He complained to the king that he had been challenged, and without checking the facts George I placed his eldest son under virtual house arrest.

..... 'You know as well as I that he is the lowest stinking coward in the world and that there is no way of gaining anything of him but by working on his fear. I know if I was asleep if that he could come behind me he is capable of shooting me through the head or stabbing me in the back.'
(Queen Caroline, wife of George II, speaking to Lord Hervey about Frederick, Prince of Wales.)

..... 'If I were to see him in Hell I should feel no more for him than I should for any other rogue that ever went there.'

(Queen Caroline about the Prince of Wales.)

'Then she may stay at home as I do. You do not see me running into every puppy's house to see his new chairs and stools. Nor is [it] for *you* to be running your nose everywhere and trotting about the town to every fellow that will give you some bread and butter, like an old girl that loves to go abroad, no matter where or whether it be proper or no.'

(To Lord Hervey and Queen Caroline deploring the habit of making frequent visits to grand houses.)

..... 'He wants to come and insult his poor dying mother but she shall not see him. No, No! He shall not come and act his silly plays here, false, lying cowardly, nauseous puppy!'

(Speaking about the Prince of Wales in 1737.)

..... 'No, I shall have mistresses.'

(Somewhat tactless reply to his dying wife, Caroline, who had advised him to marry again in 1737.)

..... 'Now, boys, for the honour of England; fire, and behave bravely and the French will soon run.'

(The king fought at the Battle of Dettingen in 1743, the last English sovereign to command an army in the field.)

..... 'The Bishop of Winchester is very modest in a canting, hypocritical knave to be crying, "The Kingdom of Christ is not of this world," at the same time that he, as Christ's ambassador, receives £6,000 or £7,000 a year . . . . Pray, what is it that charms you in him? His pretty limping gait or his nasty stinking breath? Or his silly laugh when he grins in your face for nothing and shows his nasty rotten teeth?'

(To Lord Hervey.)

..... 'I do not think that ingrafting my half-witted coxcomb upon a madwoman would mend the breed.'
(About the marriage of the Prince of Wales to a German princess.)

George III
(Born 1738; reigned 1760–1820)

The grandson of George II, he was amiable, shy, fussy and conscientious, interested in the arts and farming. He was the first of the Hanoverians to speak (and be typically) English. He remained unusually faithful to his German wife Charlotte, by whom he had a royal record of fifteen children (most of whom lived, unlike those of Queen Anne). Later in his long life he suffered from attacks of insanity and the interminable squabbles of politicians (Lord North in particular helping him to lose the American colonies.) On the credit side he had the matchless military genius of Nelson and Wellington. As usual with the Hanoverians, he had a running feud with an irresponsible eldest son.

..... 'George, be a King.'
(Exhortation from his mother, Augusta, widow of Frederick, Prince of Wales [who died in 1751], when he ascended the throne aged 22.)

..... 'You may laugh, you have been married twice. But to me it is no joke.'
(The king's bride-to-be, Princess Charlotte Sophia, to the duchess of Devonshire, the previous duchess of Manchester hence 'Double Duchess', who was travelling with her to meet the king in 1761.)

..... 'That young man has so thoroughly cast off every principle of common humour and honesty that he must become as contemptible as he is odious.'
(Letter to the Prime Minister, Lord North, in 1774, about Charles James Fox.)

..... 'We live in unprincipled days and no change can be expected but by an early attention to the rising generation.'
(To Dr Hurd, appointed tutor to the young princes in 1776.)

..... 'If they deserve it, let them be flogged; do as you used to do at Westminster.'
(Instructions from the king to his sons' tutor, the bishop of Chester. The duke of Sussex was flogged for having asthma. The king thought it his duty to be present at these punishments. Princess Sophia recalled that she had seen her two elder brothers, when they were boys of thirteen and fourteen, held by their arms to be flogged like dogs with a long whip.)

..... 'I can never suppose this country so lost to all ideas of self-importance as to be willing to grant America independence.'
(Letter to Lord North in 1780.)

..... 'I make you a present of this as a mark of the civilities we have met with on our journey today.'
(Handing Lord Onslow a stone thrown by the mob into the royal carriage during the political riots in the 1780s.)

..... 'The Prince of Wales on the smallest reflection must feel that I have little reason to approve of any part of his conduct for the last three years.'
(Letter to the Treasurer of the Prince of Wales's Household in 1783.)

..... 'When the Duke of Portland came into office I had at least hoped he would have thought himself obliged to have my interest and that of the Public at heart and not have neglected both to gratify the passions of an ill-advised young man . . . I wish I were 80 or 90 or dead.'

(After the Prime Minister and Parliament had demanded that the king discharge the debts of the profligate Prince of Wales in 1783.)

..... 'I must form a ministry from among men who know I cannot trust them and therefore will not accept office without making me a kind of slave; this undoubtedly is a cruel dilemma and leaves me but one step to take without the destruction of my principles and honour; the resigning my Crown, my dear Son to you, quitting this my native country for ever and returning to the dominions of my forefathers.'

(Letter to the Prince of Wales in 1783 contemplating abdication.)

..... 'I was the last to consent to separation, but separation having been made and having become inevitable, I have always said that I would be the first to meet friendship of the United States as an independent power.'

(To John Adams, the first US ambassador to Britain, in 1785.)

..... 'Our Saviour went about healing the sick.'

(The royal physician, Dr Willis, defending his profession against the king's strong dislike of doctors.)

..... 'Yes, yes, but he had not £700 a year for it.'

(The king's testy response to the physician's unctuous remark.)

..... 'Of all the men I have known you are the one on whom I have the greatest dependence and you are the most perfect gentleman.'

(The king talking to himself during one of his fits of madness.)

..... 'Sad stuff, only one must not say so, what, what?'

(His opinion of Shakespeare.)

..... 'Another damned thick, square book! Always scribble, scribble, scribble! Eh! Mr Gibbon?'

(The duke of Gloucester, brother of the king, when presented with the latest volume of Decline and Fall *by the author.)*

..... 'I think of him so ugly that I am sometimes obliged to turn my head away in disgust when he is speaking to me. Marry I will, and that directly in order to enjoy my liberty, but not the Prince of Orange.'

(The king's daughter, Charlotte, on her father's choice of husband for her in 1812.)

..... 'The King had taken four jellies, some cocoa and tea, is totally lost as to mind, conversing with imaginary persons, as he is constantly addressing himself to Eliza . . . 'Tis a most melancholy prospect.'

(The duke of Cumberland on the madness of his father, George III, in 1812.)

..... 'My mother was bad but she would not have become as bad as she was if my father had not been infinitely worse.'

(Princess Charlotte on her parents, the king and queen, in 1814.)

99

George IV
(Born 1762; reigned 1820–30)

Eldest son of George III, he became Prince Regent during the periods of his father's insanity from 1810 to his own accession in 1820. A voluptuary, irresponsible with money, women and drink, he was yet also 'The First Gentleman in Europe', an arbiter of taste in painting and architecture, who provided England with the nucleus of the National Gallery, Brighton Pavilion, Carlton House, the Nash Terraces in Regent's Park and a well-restored Windsor Castle. Married first illegally to Mrs Fitzherbert, a Roman Catholic, he then married (reluctantly, to settle his debts) Princess Caroline of Brunswick whom he soon sought to divorce, bringing nothing but scandal and unpopularity to the Crown. In his extravagance and licentiousness he was to be the last of his kind on the throne of England.

..... 'I shall not permit the going to balls or assemblies at private houses, which never has been the custom for Princes of Wales. As to masquerades, you already know my disapprobation of them in this country.'

(From a long letter from George III imposing limitations on the Prince of Wales [the future George IV] aged eighteen, in 1780. It was the start of a lifetime's quarrel between father and son.)

..... 'She accused me of various high crimes and misdemeanours, all which I answered and in the vulgar, English phrase, gave her as good as she brought.'

(The Prince of Wales to his brother about his mother Queen Charlotte, in 1781.)

..... 'The King was so excessively unkind . . . sometimes not speaking to me when he sees me for three weeks together, and hardly ever at Court . . .'

(The Prince of Wales to his brother Frederick in 1784.)

..... '[I have always found the day] long enough for doing nothing.'

(His reply, as Prince of Wales, to his father when reproached for late rising.)

..... 'I can as yet form no judgement of what steps can be taken as I neither know the amount to which his debts have now risen nor what security there will be that his future expenses shall be confined within his income.'

(Complaint from George III. In fact the Prince of Wales's debts at the age of 24 had reached the fearsome total of £269,878. 6s 7d in 1786.)

..... 'I am not well, pray get me a glass of brandy.'

(Cri de coeur to Lord Malmesbury on first meeting his future wife, Princess Caroline of Brunswick. The Prince of Wales embraced her then turned away. He was drunk at the wedding in 1795.)

..... 'Damn the West! Damn the East! and damn Wellington!'

(Spoken by the Prince of Wales during a discussion of the Duke's wide-ranging victories.)

..... 'I rejoice at the great and glorious news from Russia which I have, without becoming vanity, to ascribe in a great degree to my own original and indefatigable endeavours.'
(As Prince Regent, writing a totally imagined claim to his mother, Queen Charlotte, about Napoleon's retreat from Moscow in 1812. As king he later boasted that he had fought at Waterloo.)

..... 'That Spanish grandee grafted on an Irish potato.'
(As Prince Regent describing Lord Wellesley, his Foreign Secretary and brother of the duke of Wellington, in 1812.)

..... 'The King desires Lord Liverpool distinctly to understand that whatever appointments the king may think proper to make in his own family, they are to be considered as quite independent of the control of any Ministry whatever.'
(Angry reply to the Prime Minister's claim to have power to appoint a new Lord Chamberlain. The king was trying to appoint the husband of his mistress, Lady Conyngham, in 1820.)

..... 'My friends! When I arrived in this beautiful country my heart overflowed with joy,'
(On a state visit to Ireland in 1820; in fact the reason for the trip was to stay with his mistress, Lady Conyngham, at Slane Castle.)

..... 'It is the King's fixed determination to show as often as the occasion may offer the thorough disgust he feels at the unpardonable conduct of such part of his subjects as reside in the town of Dover.'
(Dover had welcomed Queen Caroline back from abroad in 1820, much to the king's displeasure.)

..... 'Caroline of Brunswick, the injured queen of England.'
(The inscription the dying queen wished to have put on her coffin in 1821. She had suffered a public trial on a charge of adultery and had later been barred from the Coronation of her husband George IV.)

..... 'I recognise his talent and I believe we need him in the Commons; but he is no more capable of conducting foreign affairs than your baby. He doesn't know the first thing about his job; no tact, no judgement, no idea of decorum.'
(Opinion of George Canning as Foreign Secretary in 1822.)

..... 'Think of that damned fellow wanting me to have the king and Queen of the Sandwich Islands to dinner, as if I would sit at table with such a pair of damned cannibals.'
(To the duke of Wellington about George Canning in 1822.)

..... 'No foreign dances. I dislike seeing anything in Scotland that is not purely national and characteristic.'
(Instructions for the Caledonian Hunt Ball in 1822.)

..... 'Either I am mad or Lord Castlereagh is mad.'
(About his Foreign Secretary in 1822. As it happened, Castlereagh killed himself shortly afterwards.)

..... 'Instead of taking him for my minister . . . I should have hanged him and eighty other rascals with him.'
(To Prince Polignac about George Canning who succeeded Castlereagh as Foreign Secretary in 1822.)

103

..... 'Good evening, sir, I suppose that you are the regimental doctor.'

(To Lord Charles Russell of the Royal Horse Guards who had appeared incorrectly dressed at a Court ball. The king was very fussy about uniforms.)

..... 'With my age and infirmity it is not worth while looking for another.'

(To the duke of Wellington about the idea of taking a new mistress after Lady Conyngham in 1826.)

..... 'Look at that idiot! They will remember me if ever he is in my place.'

(To Princess Lieven about his brother, the future William IV, in 1826.)

..... 'Arthur, the Cabinet is defunct.'

(Gloomy remark to his new Prime Minister, the duke of Wellington, in 1828.)

..... 'King Arthur must go to the Devil or King George to Hanover.'

(About the duke of Wellington, who as Prime Minister was proving inflexible, in 1828.)

..... 'Look at that idiot! Like a frog's head carved on a coconut.'

(To Princess Lieven again about his brother, shortly to be William IV, in 1830.)

William IV
(Born 1765; reigned 1830–37)

Younger brother of George IV, known as the 'Sailor King', he spent, or more accurately misspent, his early years in the Royal Navy. Later, as duke of Clarence and then king, he became a brash and cheerful extrovert, honest, sociable and straightforward, who presided (albeit sometimes unwillingly) over governments that enacted some of the most radical and reforming legislation in English history. Domestically he had the usual Hanoverian problems, fathering ten children by his long-term mistress but failing to provide an heir by his dutiful and tolerant German wife, Princess Adelaide. Nevertheless, in the words of his biographer, Philip Ziegler, 'He inherited a monarchy in tatters, he bequeathed to his heir the securest throne in Europe.'

..... 'Dullness rules here altogether but what is worse than all, not a woman fit to be touched with the tongs, not a house to put your head in after dark . . . If it were not for the duty of the ship I should perhaps hang myself.'

(As Prince William, aged 21, a naval lieutenant at Plymouth in 1786.)

..... 'My Christmas box or New Year's gift will be a family lecture for immorality, vice, dissipation and expense, and that I shall meet with the appellation of the prodigal son.'

(As Prince William, aged 22, returning to England with the Navy.)

..... 'I am sorry to say that I have been living a terrible debauched life of which I am heartily ashamed and tired. I must in the West Indies turn over a new leaf or else I shall be irrevocably ruined.'

(As Prince William, aged 23.)

..... 'I know no person so perfectly disagreeable and very dangerous as an author.'

(As duke of Clarence, aged 24.)

..... 'Lord Melville talks of passing the summer in the Highlands of Scotland but I hope he will pass it in the Tower.'

(As duke of Clarence about his old enemy who was now First Lord of the Admiralty. They had crossed swords in the Navy.)

..... 'My brother has behaved very foolishly. To be sure he has married a very foolish, disagreeable person but he should not have treated her as he has done but have made the best of a bad bargain as my father has done. He married a disagreeable woman but has not behaved ill to her.'

(As Duke of Clarence about his brother, the Prince Regent, and his father, George III, in 1796.)

..... 'Hold your potato-jaw, my dear.'

(Friendly (albeit unflattering) remark to Mrs Schwellenberg, German lady-in-waiting to Queen Charlotte, his mother.)

..... 'She is doomed, poor dear, innocent young creature, to be my wife.'

(As duke of Clarence about Princess Adelaide of Saxe-Meiningen, aged 25, when he was 52. In fact she became an ideal wife for him when he was king.)

..... 'I dined with sixteen Bishops the other day ... and humbugged them gloriously to their very heart's content. It was delightful to see how they swallowed it.'
(As duke of Clarence in 1827 on Catholic emancipation.)

..... 'There are few individuals whose career appears to His Majesty to have been more disreputable . . .'
(As king to Lord Aberdeen, the Foreign Secretary, in 1830 about the appointment of Talleyrand as French ambassador to London.)

..... 'Now, ladies and gentlemen, I wish you good night. I will not detain you any longer from your amusements and shall go to my own which is to go to bed. So, come along, my Queen.'
(Typical remark at the end of dinner at Brighton Pavilion. The king has been described by the historian Sir John Plumb as 'the most outspoken, simple, eccentric monarch of modern times'.)

..... 'Who is Silly Billy now?'
(The duke of Gloucester about his cousin, the king, during the great Reform Bill political battle in 1832.)

Victoria

(Born 1819; reigned 1837–1901)

Daughter of the duke of Kent, the younger brother of William IV, she ascended the throne aged eighteen. From an unhappy childhood she developed 'a vein of iron in her most extraordinary character'. During a century in which revolutions toppled thrones and empires Queen Victoria (first with Lord Melbourne then with Disraeli) presided over a country that expanded financially and politically into the most powerful and prosperous nation on earth. Unlike her predecessors her married life until the untimely death of Prince Albert in 1861 was happy and exemplary, although the familiar Hanoverian cycle of discord with the Prince of Wales had already begun. Latterly, although reclusive, the queen exercised considerable influence on foreign policy as 'Grandmother Europe' through the marriages of her innumerable offspring, culminating eventually in her apogee as empress of India and the extreme popular national acclaim of her Diamond Jubilee.

'I am today fourteen years old! How very old!'
   (As Princess Victoria writing in her journal on 24 May 1833.)

..... 'The boys are both very plain and have a mixture of Kalmuck and Dutch in their faces; moreover they look heavy, dull and frightened and are not at all prepossessing. So much for the Oranges, dear uncle.'
(Princess Victoria, aged seventeen, to King Leopold of the Belgians about two possible suitors [sons of the Prince of Orange] in 1836.)

..... 'I like him very much and feel confidence in him. He is a very straightforward, honest, clever and good man.'
(In her journal about Lord Melbourne on the first day of her reign in 1837.)

..... 'They wished to treat me like a girl but I will show them that I am Queen of England.'
(On the first day of her reign.)

..... 'I felt for the first time like a man, as if I could fight myself at the head of my troops.'
(Reviewing troops on horseback in Windsor Great Park in 1837.)

..... 'We were much amused by Lord Palmerston's efforts to undo a Puzzle and by his playing Spillikins with Mme de Merode; he is very agreeable and amusing.'
(At Windsor in 1837; the young queen was keen on puzzles.)

..... 'It was with some emotion that I beheld Albert – who is beautiful.'
(At Windsor on 10 October 1839.)

..... 'The last time I slept alone.'
(In her journal on the night before marrying Albert in 1840.)

..... 'You forget, my love, that I am the Sovereign and that business can stop and wait for nothing.'
(Letter to Albert who had proposed a honeymoon of more than three days in January 1840.)

..... 'I was quite furious and raged away . . . vile, confounded, infernal Tories . . . as I live I'll never forgive these infernal scoundrels with Peel at their head . . . for this act of personal spite . . . that fiend, the Bishop of Exeter.'
(Outburst by the queen over the defeat in the Commons of a Bill giving precedence to Albert over the king of Hanover in succession to the throne, in 1840.)

..... 'I, naughty man, have also been crawling after the harmless stags and today I shot two roe deer, at least I hope so, for they are not yet found.'
(Albert at Balmoral in 1848; he was a mediocre sportsman.)

..... 'Just at present I am more dead than alive from overwork. The opponents of the Exhibition work with might and main to throw all the old women into panic and to drive myself crazy.'
(Albert, the prime mover behind the Great Exhibition of 1851.)

..... 'One cannot think of this country without "the Duke", our immortal hero! In him centred almost every earthly honour a subject could possess . . . revered by the whole nation, the trusted friend of the Sovereign.'
(The queen on the death of the duke of Wellington.)

..... 'That blessed chloroform ... the effect was soothing, quieting and delightful beyond measure.'
(The queen used chloroform for the first time in 1853 for the birth of her eighth child, Leopold.)

..... 'The tremendous cheering, the joy expressed in every face, the vastness of the building with all its decoration and exhibits, the sound of the organ (with 200 instruments & 600 voices, which seemed nothing) & my beloved husband the creator of this great "Peace Festival . . ."
(In her journal on 1 May 1851, at the opening of the Great Exhibition.)

..... 'With the Prince of Wales one has to contend with an unhappy temper, incapacity of concentrating his mind and defective mental qualities.'
(To Major Elphinstone, a member of the Household, about the future Edward VII, aged twelve in 1853.)

..... 'The crowd behaved worse than I have ever seen them do and we were mobbed by all the shopboys in the town who ran and looked under my bonnet, treating us just as they do the Band when it goes to the Parade. We walked home as fast as we could.'
(Writing about a visit to Brighton in 1854. The queen sold the Pavilion to the town in 1850.)

..... 'It is that continual and unbounded dislike (in England) of foreigners and everything foreign which breaks out continually, and is very painful to the Queen – whose husband, Mother and all her dearest relations and friends are foreigners.'
(In her journal in 1854.)

111

..... 'I wish we had her at the War Office.'

(The queen expressing her great admiration for Florence Nightingale in 1856.)

..... 'The Queen has a right to claim that her husband should be an Englishman, bearing an English title and enjoying a legal position which she has not to defend with a wife's anxiety.'

(About the Parliamentary Bill to give Albert a title in 1857.)

..... 'I am sick of all this horrid business of politics and Europe in general and think you will hear of me going with my children to live in Australia.'

(In her journal in 1859.)

..... 'He takes no interest in anything but clothes and again clothes. Even when out shooting he is more occupied with his trousers than with game.'

(Albert criticising the Prince of Wales, aged 27, in 1858.)

..... 'If you were to try and deny it, she can drag you into a Court of Law to force you to own to it and there with you in the Witness Box she will be able to give before a greedy Multitude disgusting details of your profligacy . . .'

(Letter to the Prince of Wales in 1861 after the Nellie Wallace scandal while he was serving with the Army at the Curragh.)

..... 'He slept in long white drawers which enclosed his feet as well as his legs like the sleeping suit worn by small babies.'

(In her journal about Albert in 1862.)

..... 'Oh, if the Queen were a man, she would like to go and give those Russians whose word one cannot believe such a beating!'

(To Lord Beaconsfield [Disraeli] in 1878; he averted war at the Congress of Berlin. On his deathbed in 1888 Disraeli was asked if he wished the queen to visit him. 'No,' he replied, 'she'd only ask me to take a message to Albert.')

..... 'He speaks to me as if I were a public meeting.'

(The queen was never fond of Gladstone.)

..... 'What will become of the poor country when I die . . . if Bertie succeeds he would spend his life in one whirl of amusements.'

(In her journal in 1869.)

..... 'Dear, good boys but very exclusively English, and that is a great misfortune.'

(About her grandsons.)

..... 'Avoid the many evil temptations which beset all young men and especially Princes. Beware of flatterers, too great love of amusement, of races and betting and playing high . . . Alas, Society is very bad these days; what is wrong is winked at.'

(Letter to her grandson Prince George [the future George V] in 1885.)

..... 'We are not amused.'

(Allegedly said by the queen in 1889.)

..... 'The trials of life *begin* with marriage.'
(To Princess Mary ('May') of Teck before her marriage to the duke of York in 1893.)

..... 'Please understand that here is no one depressed in this house; we are not interested in the possibilities of defeat; they do not exist.'
(To A J Balfour in 1899 during the Boer War.)

The House of Saxe-Coburg & Gotha

1901–10

Edward VII
(Born 1841; reigned 1901–10)

Eldest son of Queen Victoria and Prince Albert, he spent the first 60 years of his rather rakish life as Prince of Wales, acquiring the nicknames 'Roger the First' and 'Tum-Tum', his main interests being women, food and shooting (in that order), all of which increased his weight and decreased his bank balance. Quite shrewd at being king (eventually at the age of 60), he died shortly after saying farewell to his favourite mistress, Mrs Keppel, at his bedside, something that would have shocked his supposedly more broadminded subjects today, but was tolerated by his beautiful if long-suffering queen, the Danish Alexandra.

..... 'We live in radical times and the more the People see the Sovereign the better it is for the People and the Country.'
(As Prince of Wales he wrote a letter to his mother Queen Victoria about her withdrawal from public life after the death of Albert.)

..... 'You may think I like marrying Bertie for his position but if he were a cowboy I would love him just the same.'
(Princess Alexandra in a letter to Princess Victoria of Prussia.)

..... 'And so, my Georgie boy has become a real live filthy blue-coated Picklehaube German soldier!! Well, I never thought to have lived to see that!'

(Princess Alexandra [later Queen] showing Danish dislike for Germans when her son Prince George [later George V] was given honorary command of a Prussian regiment during a state visit to Berlin in 1890.)

..... 'You can tell when you have crossed the frontier into Germany because of the badness of the coffee.'

(As Prince of Wales, quoted by Lord Haldane.)

..... 'We are all Socialists nowadays.'

(As Prince of Wales in a speech at Mansion House on 5 November 1895.)

..... 'Good morning, children. Am I not a funny-looking old man?'

(The king in his full Coronation robes to his amazed grandchildren in 1902.)

..... 'Let me introduce you to the last King of England.'

(To Lord Haldane introducing him to the Prince of Wales [later George V].)

..... 'I do not know much about Art but I think I know something about Arrangement.'

(The king rearranged the pictures and furniture at Windsor.)

..... 'Either the brute is a king or else he is an ordinary black nigger, and if he is not a king, why is he here?'
(The king insisting that King Kalakua of the Sandwich Islands should take precedence over the Crown Prince of Germany.)

..... 'It's all very interesting, Sir Henry, but you should never wear a coloured tie with a frock-coat.'
(When Sir Henry McMahon, Chief Commissioner of Baluchistan, reported at length to the king in 1907 on the troubles in India, the king listened intently before finally making this remark.)

..... 'William is a bully and most bullies when tackled are cowards.'
(About the German Kaiser whom the king never liked.)

..... 'What a silly place to build a bunker! See that this is altered tomorrow.'
(The king had golf courses laid out at Windsor and Sandringham although he did not like to be thwarted either at golf or croquet.)

..... '[He] preferred men to books and women to either.'
(Comment made about the king.)

..... 'I have no wish to pose as protector of morals, especially abroad.'
(Reply to the bishop of Ripon.)

..... 'waiters in a second-class restaurant.'
(The king's description of the Portuguese nobility.)

..... 'What tiresome evenings we shall have.'
(During mourning for the king of Denmark, his wife's father, women were excluded from Windsor for Ascot.)

..... 'Well, Lord Rayleigh, discovering something, I suppose.' [Then to a lady nearby,] 'He's always at it.'
(Lord Rayleigh was a great authority on electro-magnetism.)

. . . 'Mr Haldane, you are too fat.'
(Comment at dinner at Windsor; somewhat unfair coming from a very corpulent monarch.)

..... 'Goin' rattin', 'Arris?'
(To Lord Harris who turned up at Ascot in a brown bowler.)

..... 'What can the government be thinking of in excluding teaching of religion in schools? Do they wish to copy the French?'
(To Lord Esher in 1906)

..... 'The Foreign Office, to gain their object, will not care a pin what humiliation I have to put up with.'
(To Lord Knollys in 1908 about having to meet the Kaiser.)

..... 'I thought I could not do it; but then of course there is simply nothing one can't do.'
(Queen Alexandra visiting the very badly wounded and mutilated during World War I.)

The House of Windsor

1910–

George V
(Born 1865; reigned 1910–36)

The second son of Edward VII and Queen Alexandra, Prince George had begun a career in the Royal Navy when the sudden death of his elder brother, the duke of Clarence, in 1892 placed him in direct line to the throne. In 1893 he married Princess Mary ('May') of Teck (the wedding presents were valued at £300,000) by whom he had six children. In turn the duke of York, Prince of Wales and finally George V, he travelled widely in the British Empire, giving exemplary leadership during World War I, the General Strike of 1926, the trials of the first Labour government and the economic crisis of 1931. Basically shy albeit quick-tempered, he was, beneath his gruff, salty manner, a kind, considerate man, more at home in the royal squirearchies of Sandringham and Balmoral (he was a matchless shot). He set very high standards of monarchical 'duty', too high for his eldest son, the Prince of Wales. The Silver Jubilee of 1935 evoked a great surge of popular acclaim for a king and queen who had added considerable stability and respect, if not glamour, to the throne.

..... 'They used to make me go up and challenge the bigger boys – I was awfully small then – and I'd get a hiding time and again.'
(As Prince George he was relentlessly bullied when a naval cadet on HMS Britannia *in 1877.)*

123

..... 'Look at poor Crown Prince Rudolph. She [Princess Stephanie] was certainly too young when he married her . . . the result was he committed suicide and killed his mistress [Baroness Marie Vetsera] and brought the most terrible sorrow & shame to his poor wife and parents; that is only one instance of young marriages I know of.'

(Prince George to Queen Victoria, his grandmother, when she urged him to marry. He was referring to the notorious Habsburg scandal at Mayerling in 1889.)

..... 'Now, Georgie, don't you think you ought to take May into the garden to look at the frogs in the pond?'

(Princess Louise to her brother at Sheen Lodge to encourage the courtship that led to his marriage to Princess Mary of Teck in 1893.)

..... 'I know I am, at least I am vain enough to think that I am capable of loving anybody (who returns my love) with all my heart and soul, and I am sure I have found that person in my sweet little May.'

(Sincere and devoted expression of what was to be a life-long love, written soon after their honeymoon. He showed his affection more easily in letters than in open emotion.)

..... 'It is certainly very disagreeable to me having to go to Berlin just now & in fact anywhere abroad as they apparently all hate us like poison.'

(As duke of York in 1900 apropos European feeling about the Boer War.)

..... 'Abroad is awful. I know because I've been there.'

..... 'Everybody admires her very much which is very pleasing to me. I hope you are as proud of your daughter-in-law as I am of my wife . . . I don't think I could have done all this without her.'

(Letter to Queen Alexandra about Princess May after the first royal tour of the Far East to Australia and New Zealand in 1901. It was the prototype of all subsequent Commonwealth tours.)

..... 'I shall soon have a regiment not a family.'

(On the birth of their fifth child in 1902.)

..... 'I saw Frank several times in London; he is still busily occupied doing nothing.'

(A reference in 1906 to the duchess of York's brother, Prince Francis of Teck, a wayward young man who was expelled from Wellington College for throwing the headmaster over a hedge, served briefly in the Army (on one occasion at Porchester Races in Ireland he lost £10,000 on a single bet), and formed several unfortunate attachments to older married women, to one of whom he gave away the 'Cambridge emeralds'. His mother adored him; not so Queen Victoria. The duchess of York was the future Queen Mary, wife of George V.)

..... 'Some people are surprised that my father and I are so particular about these things. But wouldn't it be peculiar if in ordinary society people turned up with their shirts outside their trousers?'

(Edward VII and George V were meticulous about dress and decorations.)

..... 'I see that a great number of Labour members have been returned which is rather a dangerous sign, but I hope they are not all Socialists.'

(As Prince of Wales in 1906 to his father Edward VII about the General Election.)

..... 'I could not help noticing that the general bearing of the European towards the Natives was, to say the least, unsympathetic.'

(As Prince of Wales in India in 1909.)

..... 'I can't think, Sir George, how you can go on seeing that damned fellow, Lloyd George.'

(As Prince of Wales in 1909 to Sir George Murray, Permanent Secretary to the Treasury; Lloyd George was Chancellor of the Exchequer.)

..... 'The last thing he understood was when I told him his horse, Witch of Air, had won at Kempton today and he said he was pleased.'

(At the deathbed of his father Edward VII in 1910.)

Asked by the Prime Minister, Asquith, to send a congratulatory telegram to 'Old Hardy' (Thomas Hardy) on his 70th birthday in 1910, the king gave instructions and Mr Hardy of Alnwick (who made the king's fishing rods) unexpectedly received an inexplicable royal message. In fact the king read novels regularly, his favourite authors being John Buchan, Gilbert Frankau, A E W Mason, C S Forester and even Ernest Hemingway.

..... 'Rather tired after wearing the Crown for three hours; it hurt my head as it is pretty heavy.'

(After the Coronation Durbar in Delhi in 1911.)

..... 'His Majesty cannot help feeling that there is something shocking, if not almost cruel, in the operation to which these insensate women are subjected . . .'

(To the Home Secretary, Reginald McKenna, about the forcible feeding of suffragettes in 1913.)

..... 'Our spies are the worst and clumsiest in the world.'

(To Count Mensdorff, his cousin, comparing the British and German Secret Service in 1911.)

..... 'We have seen enough of the intrigue and meddling of certain ladies. I'm not interested in any wife except my own.'

(To Count Mensdorff about to the 'smart set' of his father Edward VII.)

..... 'Dull perhaps but certainly respectable.'

(Comment about his own Court.)

..... 'We sailors never smile on duty.'

(To his private secretary, Lord Stamfordham, who had encouraged him to display more public geniality in 1914.)

..... 'My God, Mr Page, what else could we do?'

(To the US Ambassador, Walter Page, on 6 August 1914, two days after the declaration of war on Germany.)

..... 'If anyone acted like that and told tales out of school he would at school be called a sneak.'
(To Lord Kitchener, War Minister in 1915, about General Haig's conduct in writing to the king behind the back of the Comander-in-Chief, Sir John French. Haig succeeded French in 1916.)

..... 'Intern me first.'
(To the Prime Minister, Asquith, in 1916 when there was a demand for wholesale internment of all aliens.)

..... 'I may be uninspiring but I'll be damned if I'm an alien.'
(Retort to H G Wells's remark about an 'alien and uninspiring court'.)

..... *In 1917 the king changed the Royal Family name to Windsor. On hearing this the Kaiser remarked that he would like to attend that popular opera,* The Merry Wives of Saxe-Coburg-Gotha.

..... 'Very often I feel despair and if it wasn't for you I should break down.'
(Written in 1918, an indication of the strain of four years of war and his continual devotion to Queen Mary.)

..... 'In all my life I have never seen a German gentleman.'
(To Franklin D Roosevelt, Under-Secretary for the US Navy in London in 1918.)

..... 'The nearest I got to the United States was when I walked half across Niagara, took my hat off and walked back again.'
(The king had no wish to visit the USA.)

..... 'My father was frightened of his mother, I was frightened of my father and I am damned well going to see to it that my children are frightened of me.'

(To Lord Derby.)

..... 'What in heaven's name is this?'

(Reaction to the appearance of an avocado at dinner; the king disliked exotic food.)

..... 'Good God, look at those short skirts, look at that bobbed hair.'

(Exclamation of disapproval made at an open window at Windsor about passing visitors, until called to order by Queen Mary.)

..... 'England is good enough for me. I like my own country best, climate or no, and I'm staying in it. I'm not like my father.'

..... 'He taught me how to be king.'

(About his private secretary Lord Stamfordham.)

..... 'Yes, and I expect they would offer me a million.'

(Remark when Field Marshal Lord Haig said he had been offered £100,000 for his memoirs in the twenties.)

..... 'Mussolini resembles a *mad dog* which must bite somebody . . .'

(To the Foreign Secretary in 1923 – an early perceptive comment.)

..... 'You are indeed a lucky man to have such a charming and delightful wife as Elizabeth ... You have always been so sensible and easy to work with ... very different to dear David.'

(Letter to the duke of York [later George VI] about the Prince of Wales [later Edward VIII] in 1924.)

..... 'You are not late, my dear, I think we must have sat down two minutes early.'

(Remarkable concession by the strictly punctual king, showing his extreme fondness for the newly married duchess of York [the future Queen Elizabeth].)

..... 'I tell you what. Turner was *mad*. My grandmother always said so.'

(A reference to Queen Victoria's opinion of the famous painter. The king preferred the work of Frith, Landseer and Winterhalter.)

..... 'He is quite wonderful but I wish he didn't have long hair.'

(Comment after a recital by the violinist Kubelik at Sandringham.)

..... 'His Majesty does not know what the band has just played but it is never to be played again.'

(After hearing the Grenadiers playing some Richard Strauss music at Buckingham Palace. However, the king made Delius a Companion of Honour.)

..... 'Stick to Shakespeare, Mr Lee, there's money in Shakespeare.'

(Advice to the author Sidney Lee at a vaguely literary dinner. Previously he had been told that another guest was an authority on Lamb. The king exclaimed incredulously: 'An authority on lamb?')

..... 'There you go again, May; furniture, furniture, furniture.'
*(To Queen Mary at dinner at Balmoral when he overheard
her talking about antiques with her godson, the aesthetic
Sir Michael Duff.)*

..... 'Did you come here expecting to eat winkles?'
*(To an unfortunate guest who dropped a hairpin in her soup at
Sandringham.)*

..... 'Make me look like a stuffed monkey, don't they?'
(Comment on a new issue of British stamps.)

..... 'Amsterdam, Rotterdam and all the other dams. Damned
if I'll do it.'
*(Reaction when asked if he would make a state visit to Holland.
He loathed travelling abroad except to the Empire.)*

..... 'Today, 23 years ago, dear Grandmama [Queen Victoria]
died. I wonder what she would have thought of a Labour
Government.'
*(Diary entry, 22 January 1924, after asking Ramsay MacDonald to
form a government.)*

..... 'I must say they all seem to be very intelligent and they
take things very seriously they ought to be given a chance and
ought to be treated fairly.'
(About the first Labour Cabinet in 1924.)

..... '[It would be a] grave mistake to do anything which might be interpreted as confiscation or to provoke the strikers who until now have been remarkably quiet.'
(Advice to the government during the General Strike in 1926.)

..... 'Try living on their wages before you judge them.'
(To Lord Durham, a very rich coalmine owner, who had called the miners 'a damn lot of revolutionaries', during the General Strike in 1926. Admittedly, in that same year Sir John Fortescue, the royal librarian, recorded that Windsor Castle was staffed by some 600 indoor servants.)

..... 'I thought people like that shot themselves.'
(On being told by the duke of Westminster that his brother-in-law, Earl Beauchamp, was homosexual.)

..... 'What could you possibly want that queer old place for? Those damned weekends, I suppose.'
(Comment in 1930 when he gave the Prince of Wales Fort Belvedere, a Victorian folly in Windsor Great Park.)

..... 'You've got us into this mess, Mr MacDonald, and you've got to get us out.'
(To the Prime Minister on forming the National Government in 1931.)

..... 'I have read your memorandum; not all of it, of course.'
(To Robert Vansittart at the Foreign Office; a hint for brevity.)

..... 'Marina has not a cent.'
(Candid comment on the engagement of the impecunious Princess Marina of Greece to Prince George [Duke of Kent] in 1934, although Queen Mary added, 'No bread-and-butter miss would be any help to my son but that girl is sophisticated as well as charming . . .' An accurate opinion, as it turned out.)

..... 'I'm a bad hand at saying what I feel.'

..... 'But of course you have no words to say, and talking is three-quarters of acting.'
(Somewhat tactless remark to Lady Diana Cooper after seeing her performance in The Miracle *when she portrayed a silent statue.)*

..... 'In the last war fortifications were useless and would be even more so in the next.'
(Very perceptive comment about the Maginot Line in 1934.)

..... 'Wake up, England!'
(Title of a book of reprinted speeches.)

..... 'Bugger Bognor!'
(Reply to a suggestion that he should recuperate again at Bognor Regis after his illness in the thirties.)

..... 'You dress like a cad. You act like a cad. You are a cad. Get out.'
(One of the many rows between the king and the Prince of Wales, particularly during the Mrs Simpson affair.)

..... 'He has not a single friend who is a gentleman.'
(About the Prince of Wales in 1934, spoken to Count Mensdorff, former Austrian ambassador.)

..... 'No more coals to Newcastle, no more Hoares to Paris.'
(Joke about the resignation of Sir Samuel Hoare as Foreign Secretary in 1935 after he had signed the infamous Hoare-Laval Pact in Paris that aimed to legitimise the Italian conquest of Abyssinia.)

..... 'I will not have another war. *I will not.* The last one was none of my doing and if there is another one and we are threatened with being brought into it, I will go into Trafalgar Square and wave a red flag myself.'
(To Lloyd George in 1935.)

..... 'I am not a clever man but if I had not picked up something from all the brains I've met, I would be an idiot.'

..... 'I'd no idea they felt like that about me. I am beginning to think they must like me for myself.'
(During a Silver Jubilee drive in 1935 through the East End of London where he was given a great reception.)

..... 'I am a very ordinary fellow.'
(To the archbishop of Canterbury on Jubilee Day in 1935.)

..... 'I pray to God that my eldest son will never marry and have children, and that nothing will come between Bertie [George VI] and Lillibet [Elizabeth II] and the throne.'
(To Lady Algernon Gordon-Lennox a few weeks before he died.)

134

..... 'When I am gone the boy will ruin himself in twelve months.'

(To Lord Derby about the Prince of Wales.)

..... 'How is the Empire?'

(Spoken on the day he died but not his last words.)

Queen Mary
(Born 1867; Queen Consort:
1910–36
Queen Mother: 1936–53)

Known as Princess 'May', she was born in Kensington Palace to the duke and duchess of Teck, impecunious minor German royalty, her mother being a cousin of Queen Victoria. Brought up mostly in England, a charming if rather shy girl, she became engaged in December 1891 to the duke of Clarence, the somewhat unstable eldest son of the Prince of Wales (later Edward VII). He died of pneumonia six weeks later and she married his brother, Prince George (later the duke of York and George V) in the following year. Tall, beautiful and in later years a stately figure, she became a popular and much loved wife, Queen and Queen Mother, a notable exemplar of royal 'duty'.

..... 'You see my parents were always in short street so they had to go abroad to economise.'
(In the 1880s the Teck family had to leave White Lodge in Richmond Park and live more economically in Italy and Austria for several years.)

..... 'We don't reverse.'
(Remark in her teens to Cynthia Asquith when somebody asked her to waltz at a tea-dance.)

..... 'Old Greville was screwed, too much wine having been unscrewed.'
(Jokey slang in a letter about a Christmas dinner party in 1888. Princess May, aged 21, was a delightful guest at country houses now that her family, still impecunious, were back in England at White Lodge.)

..... 'And now to your drive in a Motor-Car! Yes, I very nearly had a fit and quite screamed out to myself . . . Oh, dearest child, how could you?'
(Somewhat frantic response from Princess Mary's favourite aunt, Grand Duchess Augusta of Mecklenberg, aged 80, when hearing of her niece's drive in Lord Shrewsbury's car in 1903.)

..... 'of all people even Sovereigns now flying up into the air!'
(A reference by Grand Duchess Augusta to the first Zeppelin airship.)

..... 'It was so stiff I could have turned cartwheels for sixpence.'
(Remark at a shooting party; these occasions bored Princess May considerably.)

..... 'I shall be very disappointed if George doesn't come up again.'
(Droll remark when her husband, then Prince of Wales, went to sea in a submarine.)

137

..... 'I wish I were not such a snail in its shell.'
(Written during a house party of Lord Derby at Knowsley in 1906. Although now Princess of Wales, she was still rather shy of Edward VII's 'smart set'.)

..... 'You were the one who had shown proper feeling in your deportment when that horrible Bomb was thrown.'
(Letter from Grand Duchess Augusta to Princess May after an anarchist, Morales, had thrown a bomb at the Spanish king and queen on their wedding day in Madrid in 1906.)

..... 'The position is no bed of roses.'
(Candid comment on her new role as Queen Consort in 1910 in a letter to her Aunt Augusta.

..... 'Oh, that would have been my fourth [Coronation] but this I dare not think of unless some Aerobike takes me to fly across.')
(Aunt Augusta's reply to the news.)

..... 'This K.G. so startled me I quite hopped on my chair.'
(Another eccentric comment from Aunt Augusta to Queen Mary, this time when George V bestowed the Order of the Garter on her son, the duke of Mecklenburg, in 1911.)

..... 'Fancy our going kissing all over the world, but it is impossible to stop those horrid Kino-men.'
(Another testy letter from Grand Duchess Augusta of Mecklenberg, aged 90 in 1913, about the news film of her greeting her niece on a visit to Germany.)

..... 'The sunset of his death tinged the whole world's sky.'
(Diary entry by Queen Mary on the death of George V on 20 January 1936. Both the reign and the marriage had exemplified the stability of the Royal Family.)

..... 'We prefer the picture to remain as by Nollekens.'
(Very royal remark when told that one of the royal paintings was by Mercier not Nollekens.)

..... 'May I go back and say goodbye to that dear little cabinet?'
(A strong hint to her hosts from the queen, a formidable collector, that she would like to acquire the object concerned. Many such family treasures were lost to the royal collection at Windsor.)

..... 'Perhaps we should still be one country if my great-grandfather had not been so obstinate.'
(To a US visitor, referring to George III.)

Queen Mary had the habit of referring to royalty as 'Dear so-and-so' and to commoners as 'Poor so-and-so', regardless of health or fortune.

..... 'I don't like it, but the one thing that I have always feared for David is drink. I was afraid it would ruin him or make him a laughing-stock. And she [Mrs Simpson] has been a sane influence in that respect.'
(Queen Mary about the Prince of Wales in 1935. When someone later said that the duchess of Windsor had stopped him drinking – no more pouches under his eyes – 'Yes,' said Queen Elizabeth, 'who has the lines under his eyes now?' [meaning George VI].)

..... 'Well, Mr Baldwin, this is a pretty kettle of fish.'

(To the Prime Minister at Marlborough House when the Abdication Crisis broke in November 1936.)

..... 'Really, this might be Rumania.'

(Comment at the height of the Abdication Crisis. King Carol had undergone a notoriously unstable time on the throne of Rumania in the twenties and thirties. He finally abdicated in 1940.)

..... 'Then came the dreadful goodbye as he was leaving that evening for Austria. The whole thing was too pathetic for words.'

(Written after the parting with the duke of Windsor at Royal Lodge, Windsor, on the night of 11 December 1936.)

..... 'Thank God this sad year is over.'

(Written at Sandringham at Christmas 1936. There had been, uniquely, three kings on the throne in less than a year.)

..... 'It seems inconceivable to those who had made such sacrifices during the war that you, as their King, refused a lesser sacrifice.'

(Letter to the duke of Windsor in 1938. Her deep sense of 'duty' had always been paramount.)

..... 'In any other country there would have been riots; thank God people did not lose their heads.'

(Written after the Abdication.)

..... 'I travelled 1,687 miles in my car this month.'

(Very precise entry in her diary for 29 September 1938.)

..... 'We three were in a heap at the bottom of the car and we got out by the help of two ladders.'

(In 1939 her Daimler was hit by a heavy lorry and although aged 72 and severely bruised, she showed considerable calm and courage.)

On 4 September 1939 at the outbreak of war Queen Mary motored to Badminton, the home of the duke and duchess of Beaufort (her niece) with 63 staff and dependants. She stayed there until 1945.

..... 'So that's what hay looks like.'

(Remark to the somewhat surprised duchess of Beaufort. Queen Mary had lived entirely in a metropolitan world or in the secluded life of country houses like Sandringham and Balmoral.)

..... 'Oh, I have been happy here. Here I've been anybody to everybody, and back in London I shall have to begin being Queen Mary again.'

(On leaving Badminton in June 1945.)

..... 'When I die INDIA will be found written on my heart.'

(Comment in 1947 at the time of Independence, reminiscent of Mary Tudor and Calais. As Princess May she had fallen in love with India during the state visit in 1906.)

..... 'The first time Bertie wrote me a letter with the "I" for Emperor of India left out, very sad.'

(Written by Queen Mary on the back of an envelope from the king on 18 August 1947, shortly after Independence.)

..... 'Wilhelmina is only 68 and that is no age to give up your job.'

(On hearing that Queen Wilhelmina of the Netherlands was abdicating in 1948.)

..... 'Do you know there is one thing I never did and wish I had done; climb over a fence.'

(Remark in old age to her daughter-in-law Queen Elizabeth.)

..... 'Her old Granny and subject must be the first to kiss Her hand.'

(Aged 85 she went to Clarence House to do homage to her eldest granddaughter who at the age of 25 had become her sovereign.)

Edward VIII

(Born 1894; reigned Jan–Dec 1936; died 1972)

The eldest son of George V and Queen Mary, he was educated at Osborne, at Dartmouth and at Oxford, becoming Prince of Wales in 1911. He was prevented from serving in the trenches in World War I, and in the twenties embarked on a series of highly successful world tours, achieving diplomatic as well as popular acclaim. His subsequent well-publicised private life of night-clubs, mistresses and weekend parties at Fort Belvedere set him at odds with the traditional lifestyle of his father, culminating finally in his intention to marry a twice-divorced American, Wallis Simpson. His abdication in 1936 was followed by some thirty years of aimless luxury in France and the USA. From a young prospect of golden opportunity, a wayward 'Prince Charming' had managed sadly to tarnish, albeit temporarily, the lustre of the monarchy.

..... 'I have often felt that despite his undoubted affection for all of us, my father preferred children in the abstract.'

..... 'It was that, while I was prepared to fulfil my role in all this pomp and ritual, I recoiled from anything that tended to set me up as a person requiring homage.'
(His thoughts at the time of his investiture as Prince of Wales, aged seventeen, in 1911).

..... 'The Germans as a race are fat, stolid, unsympathetic, intensely military and all the men have huge cigars sticking out of their faces at all times.'

(After his visit to Germany in 1913.)

..... 'When shall I be sent out? It is terrible for me to sit here and see all my friends being killed or wounded.'

(To Lord Kitchener requesting service on the Western Front in World War I in 1915.)

..... 'My father has four sons, so why should I be fettered?'

(As Prince of Wales justifying his wish to do service in the trenches during World War I. He served briefly in the Grenadier Guards in France in 1916.)

..... 'Awful balls the whole thing. I don't think it will have much effect on the drinking community. Lloyd George forced it on Papa.'

(Comment on the king's embargo on drink at Buckingham Palace during World War I.)

..... 'I have no *real* job except that of being Prince of Wales.'

(Comment in 1915.)

..... 'I actually possess no prescribed state duties or responsibilities.'

(Comment in 1925.)

..... 'August would probably find him playing golf at Biarritz or swimming off Eden Roc or stooking wheat on his ranch in Canada. He preferred golf to yachting ... and his free evenings were more likely to be spent *en petit comité* with a few intimates at the Embassy Club than in the great houses or salons of London.'

(His own description, as Prince of Wales, of the complete break with the traditional ways of his father, George V.)

..... 'A private war with the twentieth century.'

(Comment on his father's lifestyle.)

..... 'Rot and a waste of time, money and energy.'

(Comment on state visits.)

..... 'I love you more and more every minute and no difficulties or complications can possibly prevent our ultimate happiness.'

(As Prince of Wales in 1935 to Mrs Simpson.)

..... 'What can I do? They will only say, "Here's that bloody Prince of Wales butting in".'

(To Lady Colefax in 1936.)

..... 'My brothers and sister have got large sums but I have been left out.'

(The Prince of Wales was left nothing in the will of George V. The dukes of Kent and Gloucester and Princess Mary were left £750,000 each. George VI, duke of York, was also left £750,000.)

..... 'I'll fix those bloody clocks!'
(The clocks at Sandringham had been set an hour fast by Edward VII to get everyone down early for shooting.)

..... 'Christ, what's going to happen next?'
(The new king during the funeral procession of George V in 1936 when the Maltese Cross fell off the Imperial Crown.)

..... 'Who is King? Baldwin or I? I myself wish to talk to Hitler and will do so here or in Germany. Tell him that, please.'
(To the duke of Saxe-Coburg in London in January 1936.)

..... 'The air in the room was heavy with portent.'
(Comment after the first visit of Archbishop Lang to the new king at Buckingham Palace. He was an unctuous critic of the king at the time of the Abdication.)

..... 'We have to thank the Almighty for two things: firstly that it did not rain, and secondly that the man in the brown suit's gun did not go off!'
(Lighthearted remark in a letter after the incident on Constitution Hill when an Irishman, Jerome Bannigan, pulled out a gun as the king rode past after a parade in July 1936.)

..... 'Something ought to be done . . . Something will be done.'
(Remark made during his visit to unemployed Welsh miners in November 1936, which pleased the public but not the politicians. The Press reported this as 'Something must be done.')

..... 'I refuse to be crowned with a lie on my lips.'
(The king intended to marry a divorced woman, which would have compromised his role as Head of the Church of England.)

..... 'An occupation of considerable drudgery.'
(His opinion of being king.)

..... 'Those damned red boxes, full of mostly bunk to read.'
(To Mrs Simpson about his official paperwork.)

..... 'Somehow I had the feeling that I would not be there very long.'
(The king had moved reluctantly into Buckingham Palace in October 1936.)

..... 'It was all very solemn and not a word was mine.'
(Commenting on the King's Speech with which he opened Parliament on 3 November 1936.)

..... 'They can't stop me. On the throne or off, I'm going to marry you.'
(To Mrs Simpson on 15 November 1936.)

..... 'I am going to marry Mrs Simpson and I am prepared to go.'
(To the Prime Minister, Mr Baldwin, at Buckingham Palace on 16 November 1936.)

..... 'Oh, I shan't be like Alfonso. He was kicked out. I shall go of my own accord.'

(To Duff Cooper in November 1936. Alfonso had been king of Spain.)

..... 'I'll try anything in the spot I'm in now.'

(To Mrs Simpson about a possible morganatic marriage, in November 1936.)

..... 'I'll change that. It will be the last thing I do before I go.'

(To Duff Cooper about the independence of the BBC, in November 1936.)

..... 'You can go wherever you want – to China, Labrador . . . but wherever you go I will follow you.'

(To Mrs Simpson when she offered to leave England to prevent him abdicating.)

..... 'A most appropriate place for a King making his last stand.'

(To Walter Monckton at Fort Belvedere, the king's weekend home in Windsor Great Park, on 6 December 1936, five days before he abdicated.)

..... 'I have found it impossible to carry the heavy burden of responsibility and to discharge my duties as King as I would wish to do without the help and support of the woman I love.'

(From his Abdication speech made at Windsor on 11 December 1936.)

..... 'We're going abroad, Crisp. What about the luggage?'
(To his valet on the day of his abdication.)

..... 'Never mind, I'll get you a job here.' [He then rang his brother.], 'Bertie, what about my valet, he's the best authority on medals and decorations in the world.'
(Crisp stayed on with George VI.)

..... 'It isn't possible! It isn't happening!'
(Anguished remark from the duke of Kent at Royal Lodge, Windsor, where the king went to say farewell to his mother and three brothers on the evening of 11 December 1936, before he left for France. His ancestor James II had done precisely the same thing 248 years before on 11 December 1688.)

..... 'It's very odd about George and music. You know, his parents were quite normal – liked horses and dogs and the country.'
(The duke of Windsor to Topazia Markevich, the wife of the conductor Igor, about his cousin Lord Harewood's love of music.)

..... 'I believed, among other things, in private enterprise, a strong Navy, the long weekend, a balanced budget, the gold standard and close relations with the United States.'
(As the duke of Windsor in his memoirs.)

..... 'Remembering your courtesy and our meeting two years ago, I address to you my entirely personal, simple though very earnest appeal for your utmost influence towards a peaceful solution of the present problems.'
(Telegram to Hitler on 25 August, a week before war broke out.)

..... 'I had no intention of tinkering with the fundamental rules of the Monarchy nor of upsetting the proud traditions of the Court. In truth, all I ever had in mind was to throw open the windows a little and to let into the venerable institution some of the fresh air that I had become accustomed to breathe as Prince of Wales.'

(As the duke of Windsor in his memoirs.)

George VI
(Born 1895; reigned 1936–52)

The second son of George V and Queen Mary, Prince Albert served in the Royal Navy (taking part in the Battle of Jutland) before becoming the duke of York while at Cambridge in 1920. A likeable, humorous yet shy man with a stammer (a singular drawback in public life), he was fortunate in making an extremely happy marriage to Lady Elizabeth Bowes-Lyon. Her support and the devotion of two children were invaluable during the sadly unwanted Abdication Crisis and later the six long years of war. His early death at 56, the tragic result of his unflagging regard for the responsibilities of kingship, shocked both family and nation. He was a reluctant king whose strength of will overcame many hazards, adding honour to the Crown.

..... 'Sadistic and incompetent.'
> *(His description of an early, and short-stayed, nanny.)*

..... 'When I was on top of the turret I never felt any fear of shells or anything else. It seems curious but all sense of danger and everything else goes except the longing of dealing death in every possible way to the enemy.'
> *(Letter to the Prince of Wales after Jutland where Prince Albert, his younger brother, served in the battleship HMS Collingwood as a Sub Lieutenant in 1916.)*

*At Cambridge in 1920 he was created the duke of York,
earl of Inverness and Baron Killarney.*

..... 'It took some time and no mistake.'
*(About his longish courtship of Lady Elizabeth Bowes-Lyon, in a
letter to his cousin Lord Louis Mountbatten in 1922.)*

..... 'I'll do it provided there's no damned red carpet about it.'
*(As duke of York in the twenties he was asked to carry out various
industrial tours; the Press nicknamed him the 'Industrial Prince'.)*

..... 'Elizabeth has been marvellous as usual and the people
simply love her already. I am lucky indeed to have her to
help me.'
*(Letter to the king after a visit to Northern Ireland in 1924. His luck
was to last a lifetime.)*

..... 'I wish I could have found him before, as now that I know
the right way to breathe my fear of talking will vanish.'
*(In 1926 Lionel Logue, an Australian speech therapist, began the
successful alleviation of the duke's stammer.)*

..... 'My family are no strangers to spiritualism.'
(To Lionel Logue, his speech therapist, himself a spiritualist.)

..... 'Take care of the children and the country will take care
of itself.'
*(Slogan coined during the very successful tour by the duke and
duchess of York to Australia and New Zealand in 1927.)*

..... 'There is a lovely story going about . . . that the reason of your rushing home is that in the event of anything happening to Papa I am going to bag the Throne in your absence!!!! Just like the Middle Ages . . .'

(From a letter to the Prince of Wales who hurried back from East Africa on the news of George V's grave illness in November 1928.)

..... 'Through all the anxiety she has never once revealed her feelings to any of us. She is really far too removed; she keeps too much locked up inside herself.'

(The duke of York to the Prince of Wales about their mother, Queen Mary, during the king's illness in 1929.)

..... 'I shall do my best to clear up the inevitable mess, if the whole fabric does not crumble under the shock and strain of it all.'

(Letter to Sir Godfrey Thomas on 26 November 1936 during the Abdication Crisis.)

..... 'As he is my eldest brother I had to be there to try and help him in his hour of need . . . I then had a long talk with D [Edward VIII] but I could see that nothing would alter his decision.'

(Diary entry during the Abdication Crisis in December 1936.)

..... 'I never wanted this to happen; I'm quite unprepared for it. David has been trained for this all his life. I've never seen State papers. I'm only a Naval officer; it's the only thing I know about.'

(To Lord Louis Mountbatten in 1936.)

..... 'When D and I said goodbye we kissed, parted as Freemasons and he bowed to me as his King.'
(Comment by the duke of York [George VI] on saying farewell to his brother Edward VIII at Royal Lodge, Windsor, on the night of 11 December 1936. 'That dreadful day', in his own words.)

..... 'I meet you today in circumstances which are without parallel in the history of our Country.'
(Start of George VI's address at his Accession Council of Privy Councillors at St James's Palace on 12 December 1936, the day after the Abdication.)

..... 'I am new to the job and I hope that time will be allowed to me to make amends for what has happened.'
(From his simple and modest letter to the Prime Minister written on 31 December 1936.)

..... 'I will only say this. If in the coming years I can show my gratitude in service to you, that is the way above all others that I should choose.'
(From the king's first broadcast to the nation on 11 May 1937.)

..... 'According to the papers I am supposed to be unable to speak without stammering, to have fits and to die in two years. All in all I seem to be a crock.'
(It was a measure of his growing self-confidence as king in 1937 that he could say this jokingly to the archbishop of Canterbury just before his Coronation.)

..... 'I had to tell him to get off it pretty smartly as I nearly fell down.'
(A clumsy bishop stood on the king's robes during the Coronation in 1937.)

..... 'He is so easy to get to know and never makes one feel shy. As good a listener as a talker.'
(Compliment about President Roosevelt with whom he formed a warm friendship during the royal visit to the USA in May 1939, leading to a constructive correspondence during World War II.)

..... 'There must be no high-hat business, the sort of thing my father and those of his day regarded as essential as the correct attitude – the feeling that certain things could not be done.'
(Written after the tour of North America in 1939 that had given the king greater confidence for his new concept of kingship.)

..... 'War can no longer be confined to the battlefield . . .'
(From his speech to the nation on the day war was declared, 3 September 1939.)

..... 'I wish I had a definite job like you. Mine is such an awful mixture trying to keep people cheered up in all ways, and having to find fault as well as praising them.'
(From a letter to Lord Louis Mountbatten in October 1939.)

..... 'Everyone working at fever heat except me.'
(Characteristically modest remark by the king on the day the Germans invaded Denmark and Norway, 9 April 1940.)

..... 'Let no one think that my confidence is dimmed when I tell you how perilous is the ordeal which we are facing. On the contrary, it shines in my heart as brightly as it shines in yours . . .'

(From a broadcast to the nation on Empire Day, 24 May 1940.)

..... 'The decisive struggle is now upon us. I am going to speak plainly to you, for in this hour of trial know that you would not have me do otherwise . . .'

(From the broadcast on Empire Day, 24 May 1940.)

..... 'Personally I feel happier now that we have no allies to be polite to and to pamper.'

(Letter to Queen Mary after the fall of France, expressing sentiments shared by a majority of the nation at the time.)

..... 'Tell him to do what he is told.'

(To Lord Lloyd, Secretary of State for the Colonies, about sending the uncooperative duke of Windsor to be Governor-General of the Bahamas in July 1940.)

..... 'I could not have a better Prime Minister.'

(Written at New Year 1941; the king had had initial reservations about Churchill succeeding Chamberlain in May 1940 instead of Lord Halifax.)

..... 'I feel quite exhausted after seeing and hearing so much sadness, sorrow, heroism and magnificent spirit. The destruction is so awful and the people so *wonderful* – they *deserve* a better world.'

(Letter to Queen Mary. The king and queen continually toured the bombed areas of the East End of London in 1940.)

..... 'Many and glorious are the deeds of gallantry done during these perilous and famous days.'

(From the broadcast on 23 September 1940 announcing the creation of the George Cross and the George Medal, primarily for civilian bravery and mainly designed by the king himself.)

..... 'I have been having a worrying time of late with all the criticism of Winston and his methods . . .'

(Letter to Lord Halifax [in Washington] in March 1942. There had been Press criticism of Churchill's organisation of the War Cabinet.)

..... 'I am so glad you were able to have a talk with my brother when he was in Washington. The real fact of the matter, which he does not realise, is that having occupied the throne of this country he can never live in this country as an ordinary citizen.'

(Letter to Lord Halifax about a visit of the duke of Windsor to the USA in March 1942.)

..... 'He looks a small quiet man with a feeble voice, but he is really a tyrant. He was quite polite.'

(Diary entry about meeting Molotov, the Soviet Foreign Minister, in May 1942.)

..... 'It really is a tragedy that he of all people just when he was coming into his own should have been taken from us. I shall miss him terribly as he was such a great help to me . . . we shall all miss him all our lives.'

(Letter to Edwina Mountbatten after the death in an aircraft accident of the duke of Kent, the king's younger brother, in August 1942.)

..... 'When I look back and think of all the many hours of arduous work you have put in, and the many miles you have travelled to bring this battle to such a successful conclusion you have every right to rejoice . . .'
(Letter to Churchill after the Battle of Alamein in November 1942.)

..... 'The real gem of my tour was my visit to Malta . . .'
(Letter to Queen Mary. In June 1943 the king visited the battered and besieged island to which on his own initiative he awarded the George Cross.)

..... 'To the steel-hearted citizens of Stalingrad, the gift of King George VI in token of the homage of the British people.'
(Inscription on the Sword of Stalingrad whose design the king chose. It was presented to Stalin by Churchill on 29 November 1943 at the Teheran Conference. Marshal Voroshilov then dropped it.)

..... 'I have read the letter from my brother with great care and after much thought I feel I cannot alter a decision which I made with considerable reluctance at the time of his marriage.'
(Letter to Churchill concerning the request from the duke of Windsor for the duchess, Wallis, to have the title of 'Her Royal Highness'.)

..... 'I have been thinking the matter over since our talk and I have come to the conclusion that we are going too fast.'
(Letter to Lord Louis Mountbatten in January 1944 about the possible engagement of Prince Philip of Greece and Princess Elizabeth. Prince Philip was serving in a destroyer in the Far East.)

..... 'I am thankful that Ike has been appointed here and not M.'

(Letter to Lord Louis Mountbatten in January 1944 showing the king's preference for Eisenhower and not Montgomery to be Supreme Commander for the invasion of Europe in 1944.)

..... 'You said yesterday afternoon that it would be a fine thing for the King to lead his troops into battle, as in the old days; if the King cannot do this, it does not seem right that his Prime Minister should take his place . . .'

(From a letter to Churchill about their shared wish to accompany the invading Allied Forces on D-Day, 1944. The king's secretary, Sir Alan Lascelles, had pointed out the constitutional complications if both king and Prime Minister were killed. Churchill was not easily dissuaded.)

..... 'The great host of the living who have brought us victory on this day of just triumph and proud sorrow.'

(From his broadcast on V-E Day, 8 May 1945.)

..... 'Your breadth of vision and your grasp of the essential things were a great comfort to me in the darkest days of the war . . .'

(From a letter to Churchill [they corresponded regularly during the War] after the General Election of July 1945. He offered the outgoing Prime Minister the Order of the Garter, which Churchill eventually accepted in 1955 from Elizabeth II.)

..... 'I feel burnt out.'

(Remark made during Christmas at Sandringham in 1945. Ever since reluctantly ascending the throne in 1936, the king, never a robust man, had been involved in successive crises from the abdication itself through Munich and six long years of war.)

..... 'I want it non-political and in my gift.'
(To Prime Minister Attlee in 1946 about the Order of the Garter. Since the time of George I it had become a 'political' honour. The Garter, like the Order of Merit, would henceforward be again in the gift of the Sovereign, after telling the Prime Minister 'his ideas'.)

..... 'I asked him how he liked the responsibility of a Government Dept instead of criticising it. He laughed at that. I found him easy to talk to . . .'
(To Aneurin Bevan, Minister of Health, in 1945. The king soon established a friendly working relationship with the new Labour ministers, although initially the audiences with Prime Minister Attlee included long silences, as both were shy men. Later Attlee was to say, 'Few people realise how much time and care he gave to public affairs.')

..... 'It was a great deal to give a man all at once.'
(The king created Philip Mountbatten, Baron Greenwich, earl of Merioneth and duke of Edinburgh on the eve of his wedding to Princess Elizabeth. His pay went up from eight guineas a week as a Lieutenant, RN, to £10,000 a year on the Civil List.)

..... 'You were so calm and composed during the service and said your words with such conviction that I knew everything was all right.'
(Letter to Princess Elizabeth after her wedding to Prince Philip on 20 November 1947.)

..... 'Lord Mountbatten must have concrete orders as to what he is to do. Is he to lead the retreat out of India or is he to work for the reconciliation of Hindus and Muslims?'
(Comment on the appointment of his close friend and cousin as the last Viceroy of India in 1947.)

160

..... 'I should never relish the idea of having him either on my staff or staying in my house.'
(Letter to Lord Louis Mountbatten, newly appointed Viceroy of India, about a suggestion that Sir Stafford Cripps should accompany him. Cripps was a teetotal, vegetarian Socialist.)

..... 'Why is it, Mr Piper, that it always seems to be raining when you do a sketch at Windsor?'
(Joking comment to John Piper whose style tended towards dark, brooding backgrounds.)

..... 'I like it because you can see what is going wrong.'
(Somewhat eccentric comment on ballet.)

..... 'I have never heard of a king going to a hospital before.'
(In 1948 a major operation was performed on the king at Buckingham Palace.)

.... 'You used a knife on me, now I'm going to use this one on you.'
(He later knighted Professor James Learmonth, the surgeon, by producing a sword in his bedroom during convalescence.)

..... 'Tell me, Mr MacBride, what does this new legislation make me, an undesirable alien?'
(Half-humorous comment to Eire's Minister of External Affairs when Eire left the Commonwealth in 1949.)

..... 'Stick your neck out, but don't actually pass the axe.'
(Advice to Prince Philip about a possibly controversial speech to the British Association for the Advancement of Science in 1951.)

..... 'As we drove through the gates we felt at once the calm of the place.'

(On his return to the much-loved Royal Lodge, Windsor, on 30 November 1951 after his recuperation from an operation for cancer of the lung. He died suddenly on 6 February 1952 at Sandringham after a fine winter day's shoot with friends, the sport at which he excelled.)

Queen Elizabeth

(Born 1900; Queen Consort:
1936–52
Queen Mother: 1952–2002)

The youngest daughter of the Scottish 14th earl and countess of Strathmore, a girl of beauty and vivacious charm, she had many admirers before marrying (after a two-year courtship) the duke of York in 1923. They embarked on several successful world tours, her devoted support enabling the shy and hesitant duke to fulfil the stressful ceremonials. Later during the Abdication Crisis and particularly during the strains of World War II she not only shared the burdens of the king but established in her own right a personal popularity and admiration. The two princesses completed the happy reality of a Royal Family. Despite the tragic early death of the king, Queen Elizabeth continued a life of vigorous and varied public duties as well as her favourite relaxations on the salmon river and on the racecourse. This humorous, charming, determined lady reached an unprecedented pinnacle of popularity and affection, a devoted family figure and the most renowned of great-grandmothers.

..... 'How do you do, Mr Ralston? I haven't seen you look so well, not for years and years.'

(*As Lady Elizabeth Bowes-Lyon, aged four, to the factor at Glamis Castle.*)

..... 'SOSLSDRSVP'
(Telegram to her father, the earl of Strathmore, asking for more pocket money as a schoolgirl.)

..... 'Dear David, I hope your affairs are going well, and that neither your heart nor your staff are giving you cause for worry. These two seem to give you most trouble in life, and also of course you are very, very naughty, but delicious.'
(From a letter when she was duchess of York to the Prince of Wales [future Edward VIII] in 1923. At this time they were very good friends.)

..... 'If there have to be gentlemen waiting outside my bedroom door, I hope it's someone we know . . .'
(As duchess of York in 1930 awaiting the birth of Princess Margaret. The archaic custom of the Home Secretary attending a royal birth was discontinued by George VI.)

..... 'Mr John was quite cross because I had been on holiday and had changed colour.'
(Augustus John never managed to finish her portrait, which nevertheless was still a favourite at Clarence House. Her private collection included the work of Nolan, Drysdale, Lowry, Monet, Sisley and her friend Edward Seago.)

..... 'It is difficult to know when not to smile.'
(Comment, as duchess of York in 1937, about being photographed.)

..... 'We very nearly hit a berg the day before yesterday and the poor Captain was nearly demented because some kind cheerful people kept reminding him that it was about here that the *Titanic* was struck and just about the same date.'

(In a letter to Queen Mary in May 1939 the queen made light of the arctic weather encountered by the Empress of Australia *carrying the king and queen on their state visit to Canada and the USA.)*

..... 'I do not advise you to read it through, or you might go mad, and that would be a great pity. Even a skip through gives one an idea of his mentality, ignorance and obvious sincerity.'

(After reading Hitler's Mein Kampf *the queen sent a copy to Lord Halifax, the Foreign Secretary, with a note in November 1939.)*

..... 'I'm glad we've been bombed. It makes me feel I can look the East End in the face.'

(Buckingham Palace was bombed on 9 September 1940. The East End of London was to take the brunt of the bombing.)

..... 'The children could not go without me, and I could not possibly leave the King – who would never go.'

(Queen Elizabeth in 1940 about a suggestion that the princesses should be sent to Canada for safety.)

George VI was always referred to as 'the king' never 'the late king'.

..... 'The chopper has changed my life as conclusively as that of Anne Boleyn.'

(A keen air traveller, she found helicopters to be invaluable in the fifties.)

165

..... 'I am delighted to tell you that today I took over as first pilot of the Comet aircraft.'

(A telegram she sent in 1955 to the RAF squadron of which she was Honorary Air Commodore.)

..... 'I know where the flies go in winter time.'

(She occasionally liked to sing old-fashioned songs like this one on picnics in the heathery Scottish privacy of Balmoral.)

..... 'There is all the difference in the patient's meaning of the word and the surgeon's.'

(Wry comment on the bulletin issued by her surgeon, Sir Ralph Marnham, stating that she was 'comfortable' after an operation in 1966.)

..... 'I think you will find the Hilton is very much nicer if you look at it upside down. Modern architecture is much better seen this way.'

(A view not unlike that of her grandson Prince Charles.)

..... 'I give you a toast: Idi Amin, President Carter and Wedgwood Benn.'

(Joking allusion to some of her less favourite people. President Carter had once kissed her on the lips – a major gaffe.)

..... 'You are getting rather bloodthirsty, Dick.'

(Literary criticism: she was a regular reader of the novels of Dick Francis, her former jockey.)

..... 'Is that wise? You know you have to reign all afternoon.'
(Lighthearted comment to her daughter who was drinking wine one lunchtime at Clarence House.)

..... 'This is how you do it, it is like opening a huge jar of sweets.'
(Explaining to Prince Charles how to wave to crowds.)

..... 'Work is the rent you pay for life.'
(Reply to the queen's suggestion that she lessen her engagements when in her eighties.)

..... 'The Salmon's Revenge.'
(Joking remark at the age of 82 when she suffered considerable shock when a salmon bone stuck in her throat, necessitating admission to hospital. She had a lifelong skill at salmon fishing.)

..... 'We always took Dickie with a pinch of salt.'
(Comment on the ubiquitous Lord Louis Mountbatten.)

... 'We are lucky with Archbishop Runcie, he is such a good egg.'

..... 'Tell those old queens downstairs that this old Queen would like tea.'
(Humorous comment on the footmen at Clarence House.)

..... 'I'm afraid I don't awfully care for yours do you mind if I supply my own?'
(About the candles for her lying-in-state. She had planned her funeral in great detail.)

Prince Philip
Duke of Edinburgh
(Born 1921–)

Born on the island of Corfu to Prince Andrew and Princess Alice of Greece, a great-great-grandson of Queen Victoria (through the Battenbergs), he was educated at Gordonstoun and Dartmouth. In 1947, while serving in the Royal Navy, he married Princess Elizabeth (a remote cousin), having acquired British citizenship. After her accession he developed interests in science, the technology of industry and conservation, travelling more than 75,000 miles and making some 50 major speeches on average each year. He also dropped the occasional well-publicised brick. A hardworking, determined, often humorous and sometimes outspoken prince, husband and father, he has fulfilled the difficult role of Royal Consort skilfully and done much to modernise both the image and the workings of the monarchy.

..... 'A discredited Balkan prince of no particular merit or distinction.'
(About himself. Actually he is a Greek prince of Danish origin.)

..... 'I certainly never felt nostalgia about Greece. A grandfather assassinated and a father condemned to death does not endear me to the perpetrators.'
(George I was assassinated in 1913, Prince Andrew condemned to death by the revolutionary junta in 1923 then sent into exile.)

..... 'Left to my own devices I'd have gone into the Air Force without a doubt.'

(The family tradition of the Mountbattens tilted him towards the Royal Navy.)

..... "I made the serious mistake of underestimating my wife's interest in horses."

(Stationed in Malta in 1949 he realised that taking up polo would mean seeing more of his wife than, say, playing cricket.)

..... 'The art world thinks of me as an uncultured, polo-playing clot.'

(In fact painting is one of his pastimes.)

..... 'I want to assure you that I have no intention of being a sitting tenant in the post.'

(As President of the National Playing Fields Association in 1949.)

..... 'This ridiculous and unhygienic custom.'

(Description of the habit of whitening the wigs of the royal footmen with a mixture of starch, flour and soap. It was discontinued.)

..... 'An amoeba – a bloody amoeba.'

(Testy description of himself when the Cabinet decided against the use of the royal surname of Mountbatten instead of Windsor at the time of the Coronation in 1952.)

..... 'Because she's the Sovereign everyone turns to her. If you have a King and a Queen, there are certain things people automatically go to the Queen about. But if the Queen is also the *Queen*, they go to her about everything.'

(Prince Philip to Basil Boothroyd.)

..... 'I don't think so. Unless it farts and eats grass she's not interested.'

(Reply to the test pilot during an early flight in the Comet in the fifties when he was asked if the queen would like to inspect the flight deck.)

..... 'Ah, I see that the pubs have just closed.'

(Comment on the late arrival of the Press during the Australian tour in 1954.)

..... 'This will remind me not to blot my copybook.'

(When presented with a blotter at Melbourne University in 1954. He has not always succeeded – like most of his fellow citizens.)

..... 'All these chaps ever want is the moment when they catch you picking your nose.'

(About Press photographers.)

..... 'What we lack is not artistic craftsmen but artistic engineers. There is no reason whatsoever in this day and age why we should be palmed off with second-rate stuff on the excuse that it is machine-made.'

(From a speech to the Convocation of the Royal College of Arts in 1955.)

..... 'Deep but narrow.'
(Comment to Peter Parker in 1956 when it was suggested that T S Eliot might be a speaker at the First Commonwealth Study Conference, of which he was President.)

..... 'The point has always seemed to be to find ways to use my position to be constructive. I am not surprised that others cannot see this; they have never been in my position!!'

..... 'Well, a lot of people prefer *Hamlet* without the Prince. Very unstable fellow, the Prince.'
(Riposte to being told – hardly originally – that a meeting of the Industrial Society in the fifties would be like Hamlet *without the Prince.)*

..... 'You might ask whether all this rushing about is to any purpose. Am I just doing it to make it look as if I'm earning my keep, or has it any national value?'

..... 'Those bloody lies that you people print to make money. These lies about how I'm never with my wife.'
(To the Press on a rumoured rift in the family; he had been away for four months on a Commonwealth tour in 1957.)

..... 'Which are the monkeys?'
(At Gibraltar when confronted by the Press and the famous apes.)

..... 'I try to say something which I hope might be interesting or at least constructive. To do this and at the same time avoid giving offence can sometimes be a ticklish business. I have come to the conclusion that when in doubt it is better to play safe – people would rather be bored than offended.'

(Introduction to his second volume of speeches [1956–9].)

..... 'I think it is about time we pulled our fingers out.'

(At a luncheon for British industrialists in October 1961.)

..... 'A bloody awful newspaper. It is full of lies, scandal and imagination. It is a vicious newspaper.'

(Spoken in 1962 about the Daily Express *when Beaverbrook was still carrying on a vendetta against the Mountbattens.)*

..... 'Don't look so sad, Sausage.'

(Quip to the queen before a public speech when he thought the microphones were not yet switched on.)

..... 'I don't like to be "Highnessed". Just call me "Sir". This is the twentieth century. You're not at King Arthur's Court, you know.'

(Remark to an over-respectful visitor.)

..... 'We may have to move into smaller premises.'

(Quip in 1969 on US television implying that the Royal Family were going 'into the red' because the Civil List had not been raised for seventeen years.)

..... 'That looks to me like something to hang a towel on.'
(About Victor Pasmore's 'Relief Construction' in the San Francisco Museum of Art.)

..... 'Friendship is such a personal and unpredictable quality. It's not based on careful assessment and it seldom comes in for analysis.'
(From a personal tribute to his friend the Maharaja of Jaipur.)

..... 'What is unique about this regiment? I will tell you. It is the only one in which the Colonel is legally married to the Colonel-in-Chief.'
(Humorous reference to his undefined role as Royal Consort. A previous remark was:)

..... 'Constitutionally I don't exist.'

..... 'One of the things about the Monarchy and its place and one of its great weaknesses is that it has to be all things to all people and of course it cannot do this . . .'
(Addressing the Foreign Press Association at a luncheon in 1964. He was indicating the difficulty of trying to please the traditionalists and the reformers, etc.)

..... 'Come to think of it, only the English would think of carrying a hat on a stick at a ceremony of State.'
(Comment on the bizarre spectacle of the Cap of Maintenance being carried on a stick at the State Opening of Parliament.)

..... 'I declare this thing open – whatever it is.'
(Slight lapse when he forgot the name of a building in Vancouver during the 1969 tour of Canada. The East Annexe to the City Hall is now known as the 'East Thing'.)

..... 'If at any stage people feel it has no further part to play, then for goodness' sake let's end the thing on amicable terms without having a row about it.'
(Comment made in Ottawa in 1969 on the relationship between the Crown and the Dominions.)

..... 'A bit of a silly joke.'
(Description of Freemasonry; he is a mason like several members of the Royal Family.)

..... 'No society that values its liberty can do without the freedom to report on, comment on, discuss and indeed gossip about people, institutions and events.'
(Despite his ambivalent attitude to the Press he has encouraged the reporting and televising of royal events.)

..... 'Well, what would I do, sit around and knit?'
(To a suggestion that he ease up a little on the round of official engagements.)

..... 'Fundungus.'
(His word for meaningless trappings.)

..... 'I take your point about models. How would you react to the suggestion that the Zoo could be run more cheaply if the exhibits were all stuffed animals?'

(Ironic reply to Sir Solly Zuckerman who had suggested that models of historically interesting ships would be a cheaper arrangement for the Maritime Trust, which aimed to preserve the real thing.)

In Peking in 1986 he joked with a British student about becoming 'slit-eyed' if he studied too long in China. Something of an old chestnut among China hands (like the 'round eyes' joke among Hong Kong Chinese), it reverberated back in Britain as yet another gaffe.

..... 'Are you sure you want to go through with this?'

(To Jomo Kenyatta just before the ceremonial of Kenya's Independence in 1963.)

..... 'What do you gargle with, pebbles?'

(To the singer Tom Jones.)

..... 'I suppose you are the head nit.'

(To the managing director of a Manchester knitting company.)

..... 'It looks like a tart's bedroom.'

(Comment on the duchess of York's interior decoration plan for her new house.)

..... 'I'm not one of the corgis.'

(To the sultan of Oman.)

..... 'You make it sound as if I were deliberately plotting to upset everyone. This happens quite by chance. In fact, most things I get kicked in the teeth about happen by chance.'

..... 'I may sound frightfully well-informed about this. But it's all based on a children's lecture I heard last year at the Royal Institution.'
(Disarming remark during a visit, as Chancellor, to Cambridge University in 1990.)

Elizabeth II
(Born 1926; reigned 1952–)

Elder daughter of George VI and Queen Elizabeth (as the duke and duchess of York) she was born in the London home of her grandparents, the earl and countess of Strathmore. At the age of ten she suddenly became heir presumptive to the throne on the abdication of her uncle Edward VIII. Soon afterwards the war virtually removed her and her sister from public life to the safety of Windsor Castle. At eighteen she was allowed to join the ATS in 1944 and three years later she married Prince Philip of Greece, then serving in the Royal Navy. Becoming queen at the age of 25 on the sudden death of her father, she began the fulfilment of what on her 21st birthday she had declared: 'That my whole life, whether it shall be long or short, shall be dedicated to your service.' Few in the Commonwealth and Britain would consider that she has failed in that considerable task. A very rich woman with four palatial homes, she has nevertheless spent more than 50 years studying state papers, consulting nine different Prime Ministers, to give her a unique insight into the affairs of the nation. Her firm, amiable personality and a strong devotion to her family have made her popular and an exemplar of stability in an age of unpredictable change. Although a natural conservative, the queen has gradually encouraged the breezes of modernity and informality to blow through the mustier corridors of both palace and protocol.

..... 'I think Uncle David wants to marry Mrs Baldwin, and Mr Baldwin doesn't like it.'
(Princess Elizabeth, aged ten, giving her own explanation of the Abdication Crisis of Edward VIII to her sister Margaret.)

..... 'We know, every one of us, that in the end all will be well . . . My sister is by my side and we are both saying goodnight to you.' (*Princess Margaret, aged ten, added* 'Goodnight and good luck to you all.')
(Princess Elizabeth's radio broadcast during Children's Hour *on 13 October 1940 in the middle of the Blitz.)*

..... 'Are we too happy?'
(Princess Elizabeth, aged fourteen, living safely with her sister at Windsor in 1940, showing concern about the continual bombing of nearby London.)

..... 'Believe it or not, I lie in my bath before dinner and think, oh, who am I going to sit by and what are they going to talk about? I'm absolutely terrified of sitting next to people in case they talk about things I have never heard of.'
(Princess Elizabeth, aged nineteen, to a friend.)

..... 'Now I realise what must happen whenever Papa and Mummy go anywhere. It's something I'll never forget.'
(As an eighteen-year-old subaltern in the ATS in 1944 she saw the absurd spit-and-polish required for a royal visit.)

..... 'I declare before you all that my whole life, whether it shall be long or short, shall be dedicated to your service.'
(From her speech to the Commonwealth at Capetown as Princess Elizabeth on her 21st birthday during the royal tour of South Africa in 1947.)

..... 'You open that one, darling.'
(To Prince Philip, indicating their wedding present from the state of Queensland – 500 cases of tinned pineapple, something of a treat in 1947.)

..... 'Those greybeards in satin breeches.'
(Comment about some Court officials when she ascended the throne.)

..... 'I'll be all right. I'm as strong as a horse.'
(Her comment when it was suggested she might take a brief rest during the long Coronation service.)

..... 'Have you seen *The King and I*?'
(Her couturier Sir Hardy Amies asked this once somewhat absent-mindedly.)

..... 'The King and *who*, Mr Amies?'
(The queen replied coolly).

..... 'There was this enormous man. I couldn't make him smaller so I had to reach up with the sword. I heard a rippling noise and my sleeve got torn.'
(Recounting one of the pitfalls of an investiture.)

..... 'It is my resolve that under God I shall not only rule but serve. This describes, I believe, the modern character of the British Crown.'

(Opening the Australian Parliament in February 1954.)

..... 'I hate honouring people wearing glasses.'

(This quirk entailed a somewhat eccentric requirement for those attending investitures in 1954.)

..... 'Much was asked of my father in personal sacrifice and endeavour. He shirked no task, however difficult, and to the end he never faltered in his duty.'

(Spoken at the unveiling of the memorial statue to George VI in The Mall in 1955.)

..... 'We live over the shop.'

(Remark exemplifying the Royal Family's mixed feelings about living in Buckingham Palace. Prince Philip set about modernising the archaic kitchens, etc.)

..... 'I am not going out for a holiday but to work.'

(The queen's reply to a suggestion that the number of people she had to meet on her 1959 Canadian tour be reduced.)

..... 'Dog-leads cost money.'

(Rebuke to Prince Charles as a child being sent back to recover a dog-lead he had dropped in the grounds. The Royal Family have been relatively thrifty since Queen Victoria's reign.)

..... 'Granny's chips.'
*(The queen's name for two pieces of jewellery belonging to Queen
Mary.)*

..... 'Get out my thing, would you?'
*(Request to her personal maid, Bobo MacDonald, to fetch her
favourite large diamond clip.)*

..... 'I knocked one off on V-E Day.'
*(Mildly surprising remark to Hammond Innes about policemen's
helmets. As Princess Elizabeth she was nineteen at the time.)*

..... 'Well, that was a fair-to-average stupid thing to do.'
(Familiar reprimand for silly mistakes.)

..... 'I don't always want to be gazing at my own cypher.'
(Comment on the design for yet another dinner service.)

..... 'Between us, we are going to many parts of the world . . .
We have no plans for space travel at the moment.'
*(By 1959 the Christmas television broadcast had acquired a
less formal touch.)*

..... 'Now it's my turn to see you make a pig of yourself.'
*(Humorous comment to a guest on her left who had watched her
eating asparagus while he waited to be served.)*

..... 'That's the most pompous thing I have ever heard.'
(The queen to the editor of the News *of the World when he asked why the Princess of Wales couldn't send a servant to buy sweets at Highgrove. The Press had hounded her, and the queen had subsequently invited twenty editors to Buckingham Palace to discuss the publicity problem.)*

..... 'You are almost the same age as my mother and there's no stopping you.'
(Teasing remark to Dr Hastings Banda, president of Malawi, and a long-time acquaintance. She enjoys meeting the somewhat unconventional Commonwealth heads of state.)

..... 'Now then, with teeth or without?'
(Her opening remark on entering the room to sit for a portrait.)

..... 'The trouble is that women are expected to be smiling all the time; it is terribly unfair. If a man looks solemn it is automatically assumed he is a serious person, concentrating with grave things on his mind.'

..... 'What Philip calls "one silly mug put on another".'
(The queen apparently loathed Jubilee mugs. The Silver Jubilee in 1977 was a great success.)

..... 'I gave up trying to stop him years ago.'
(On the outspokenness of Prince Philip.)

..... 'We'll go quietly.'
(Joking about the possibility of Britain becoming a republic.)

..... 'I think everyone will concede that today of all occasions I should begin my speech with "My husband and I".'
(The queen herself mocking the royal cliché at a Guildhall luncheon for her silver wedding anniversary in 1972.)

..... 'I speak to you as the direct descendant of George III . . . the last crowned sovereign to rule this country.'
(The queen's first words as she stepped on to US soil for the bicentennial celebrations in 1976.)

..... 'No, I am here to see the people, not the scenery.'
(Declining a visit to the Arctic Circle on a tour of Finland in 1976.)

..... 'We might well expect it to have four feet.'
(Joking reference to the first pregnancy of the equestrian Princess Anne in 1977.)

..... 'Of course, I'm a farmer myself.'
(Half-humorous comment when inspecting a prize-winning bull called Karl Marx at an agricultural fair in Lusaka, Zambia, in 1979.)

..... 'Keep your cameras trained; you may see the biggest walk-out of all time.'
(To the Press photographers when King Hassan of Morocco, inexplicably ill-mannered, abandoned the queen during a trip to the Atlas Mountains. The whole tour in 1980 was an ordeal for the royal party, although the queen publicly controlled her anger.)

..... 'Go away. Can't you leave us alone?'
(Uncharacteristic outburst by the queen at Sandringham on New Year's Eve 1980.)

..... 'Well, at least he hasn't got his father's ears.'
(Joking remark when Prince William was born, on 21 June 1982.)

..... 'With your prayers and your help and the love and support of my family I shall try to help you in the years to come . . .'
(Pleadging herself anew to her subjects in the Christmas broadcast of 1991.)

..... 'I can't understand my children.'
(At Sandringham, Christmas 1991, a propos the separation of the duke and duchess of York.)

..... 'We used to have tea there when we were small children. He was the most wonderful storyteller.'
(Said about J M Barrie in the Library at Windsor to Neil and Glenys Kinnock in 1991.)

..... 'I am quite sure that people try to do their jobs or the best they can even if the result is not entirely successful . . .'
(From a rather sad speech at London's Guildhall in November 1992 (four days after the fire at Windsor Castle) at a luncheon to mark her 40th year [the 'annus horribilis'] on the throne.)

..... 'What have we done to become such bogeymen to our daughters-in-law?'
(Question asked by the queen and Prince Philip in 1995.)

..... 'Considered inaction.'
(Her strategy for minimising the damage done to the monarchy by the royal divorces and family rows in 1996.)

..... 'I think you'll find that idea was tried out and rejected.'
(Tactful way of dealing with the odder notions of a Prime Minister at the weekly audience. Dealing with nine of them over 50 years has left her very well informed.)

..... 'Occasionally you can put your point of view, which they hadn't seen from that angle . . .'
(A propos the Prime Minister's weekly audience with the queen.)

..... 'Being rather remote, it gives one an idea of what's worrying people and how they think I can help, and sometimes I can help . . .'
(The queen receives 200-300 letters a day.)

..... 'Audiences are my way of meeting people without anyone else listening.'

..... 'I'm always fascinated by the people who come and the things they have done.'
(About investitures.)

..... 'I thought it was one of Harry's jokes?'
(Remark after the incident at Prince William's 21st birthday party, 2003)

..... 'I can't write it any other way.'
(Surprised reply to a bishop who gushed about her diary, saying
'You write it in your own hand?')

..... 'People don't seem to mind my horse trips . . .'
(Comment on her occasional visits to foreign studs. Although very
knowledgeable about and keen on horses, the queen is no longer
one of the leading owners, having around twenty mares to the
al-Maktoum brothers' five hundred. She does not bet and, contrary
to rumour, neither did the Queen Mother.)

..... 'I know how much my father loved it . . .'
(Sandringham, built by her great-grandfather Edward VII, is very
much a family home.)

..... 'married to a farmer and having lots of horses, cows and
dogs.'
(At Balmoral, her family home in Scotland, she can pretend to live
her childhood dream.)

..... 'It's nice to be able to sleep in the same bed for six weeks.'
(Another advantage of summer holidays at Balmoral.)

..... 'nobody ever tells me anything.'
(In fact the queen has been kept well-informed over the years, not
least by her dresser, her page and her financial advisor.)

The death of the Queen Mother and Princess Margaret ('us three') has meant that the queen relies more than ever on Prince Philip. It is said that she harbours an unrealisable dream of a valley in the beautiful forest of Bowland in Lancashire where 'Philip and I would like to retire . . .'